MIMESIS
INTERNATIONAL

POLITICS
n. 11

INTERREGNUM

Between Biopolitics and Posthegemony

Edited by
Giacomo Marramao

© 2020 – Mimesis International
www.mimesisinternational.com
e-mail: info@mimesisinternational.com

Isbn: 9788869772610
Book series: *Politics*, n. 11

© MIM Edizioni Srl
P.I. C.F. 02419370305

The publisher and the editor remain available to fulfill their obligations regarding the images included in the text.

TABLE OF CONTENTS

Giacomo Marramao
TOWARDS A NEW CONCEPT OF THE POLITICAL   7

SECTION 1
THE LONG SHADOW OF LEVIATHAN

Gareth Williams
IN THE WAKE OF LEVIATHAN   35

Alberto Moreiras
HEGEMONY AND KATAPLEXIS   49

Emanuela Fornari
CRISIS OF HEGEMONY: BETWEEN POPULISM AND NEOLIBERALISM   61

Jorge Álvarez Yagüez
LIMITS OF THE CONCEPT OF HEGEMONY   69

SECTION 2
THE SUBJECTS AT THE TIME
OF POSTDEMOCRACY

Roberto Esposito
POSTDEMOCRACY AND BIOPOLITICS   87

Gerardo Muñoz
NOT ALL-DEMOCRACY. POSTHEGEMONY AND THE CRISIS OF
CONSTITUTIONALISM   97

Enrica Lisciani Petrini
ON THE PARADIGM OF "SUBJECT"   111

Yoandi Cabrera
BETWEEN THE AFFECT AND THE HABITUS   123

SECTION 3
PEOPLE, COMMUNITY, MULTITUDE

Teresa M. Vilarós
THE ELEPHANT AND THE SOVEREIGN ALL OVER AGAIN   133

Humberto González Núñez
NEITHER PEOPLE NOR MULTITUDE.
POSTHEGEMONY AND THE END OF THE POLITICS OF REPRESENTATION   149

Maddalena Cerrato
BEYOND THE COMMUNITY   161

Peter Baker
POLITICS OF THE MULTITUDE   177

GIACOMO MARRAMAO
TOWARDS A NEW CONCEPT OF THE POLITICAL

Prologue. Why Interregnum?

"Interregnum" here serves as a metaphor for the suspended time that characterises our present. The term was "originally used to denote a time-lag separating the death of one royal sovereign from the enthronement of the successor". This meaning was then transposed and applied to a stalemate situation between the "no longer" of the old, dying order and the "not yet" of a new order struggling to come into being.

The primary stage for this transfer, which is widely referred to yet little understood in its actual meaning, is represented by a compelling reflection that Antonio Gramsci provides in his *Prison Notebooks*:

> That aspect of the modern crisis which is bemoaned as a "wave of materialism" is related to what is called the "crisis of authority". If the ruling class has lost its consensus, i.e. is no longer "leading" but only "dominant", exercising coercive force alone, this means precisely that the great masses have become detached from their traditional ideologies, and no longer believe what they used to believe previously, etc. The crisis consists precisely in the fact that the old is dying and the new cannot be born; in this interregnum a great variety of morbid symptoms appear. N.B. this paragraph should be completed by some observations which I made on the so-called "problem of the younger generation" —a problem caused by the "crisis of authority" of the old generations in power, and by the mechanical impediment that has been imposed on those who could exercise hegemony, which prevents them from carrying out their mission. The problem is the following: can a rift between popular masses and ruling ideologies as serious as that which emerged after the war be "cured" by the simple exercise of force, preventing the new ideologies from imposing

themselves? Will the interregnum, the crisis whose historically normal solution is blocked in this way, necessarily be resolved in favour of a restoration of the old? Given the character of the ideologies, that can be ruled out—yet not in an absolute sense.[1]

Renowned commentators (especially historians, but also some philosophers) have been captivated by the most evocative expressions used in this passage, such as the reference to the "morbid symptoms" (*fenomeni morbosi*) manifesting themselves in this stagnant backwash in the movement of history. However, they have overlooked the most significant and meaningful core of Gramsci's reflection: the idea of the "crisis of authority" of a power no longer capable of "leading" but only of "dominating". Yet this is a crucial insight: it is as though Gramsci had, on the unstable ridge of an interlude in the dynamics of history, laid the foundations for a "post-hegemonic" view through this thought, opening up a field of tension between power and authority. I will

---

1 A. Gramsci, Quaderni del carcere, Edizione critica dell'Istituto Gramsci, ed. by Valentino Gerratana, Vol. I, *Quaderni 1-5 (1929-1932)*, Einaudi, Torino 1975, Q 3 (XX), § 34 (Passato e presente), p. 311; here quoted after A. Gramsci, Selections from the Prison Notebooks, ed. and trans. Quentin Hoare and Geoffrey Nowell Smith, London: Lawrence & Wishart, 1971, p. 276. [Original text: "L'aspetto della crisi moderna che viene lamentato come «ondata di materialismo» è collegato con ciò che si chiama «crisi di autorità». Se la classe dominante ha perduto il consenso, cioè non è più «dirigente», ma unicamente «dominante», detentrice della pura forza coercitiva, ciò appunto significa che le grandi masse si sono staccate dalle ideologie tradizionali, non credono più a ciò in cui prima credevano, ecc. La crisi consiste appunto nel fatto che il vecchio muore e il nuovo non può nascere: in questo interregno si verificano i fenomeni morbosi più svariati. A questo paragrafo devono essere collegate alcune osservazioni fatte sulla cosí detta «quistione dei giovani», determinata dalla «crisi di autorità» delle vecchie generazioni dirigenti e dal meccanico impedimento, posto a chi potrebbe dirigere, di svolgere la sua missione. Il problema è questo: una rottura cosí grave tra masse popolari e ideologie dominanti come quella che si è verificata nel dopoguerra, può essere «guarita» col puro esercizio della forza che impedisce a nuove ideologie di imporsi? L'interregno, la crisi di cui si impedisce cosí la soluzione storicamente normale, si risolverà necessariamente a favore di una restaurazione del vecchio? Dato il carattere delle ideologie, ciò è da escludere, ma non in senso assoluto."]

be focusing on this motif in the final pages of this introductory essay. For the time being, it is important not to lose sight of the position of the interregnum within a diagnostic category for the present that is marked by the pair of elements called the "wave of materialism" and "crisis of authority". The interregnum, then, does not depend on a crisis of apparatuses and structures, but rather on a crisis that is at once cultural and systemic, and in which the objective element and the subjective entail each other, leading to the survival of a *power without authority*: a power reduced to mere "domination".

Zygmunt Bauman explicitly latches onto this text by Gramsci in a 2012 essay with an almost programmatic title: "Times of Interregnum".[2] Quite reasonably, he draws inspiration from Gramsci's diagnosis in order to bring it up-to-date in relation to the conditions of our time, marked by the loss of the modern triad of State-Territory-Sovereignty:

> The old order founded until recently on a similarly 'triune' principle of territory, state, and nation as the key to the planetary distribution of sovereignty, and on power wedded seemingly forever to the politics of the territorial nation-state as its sole operating agency, is by now dying. Sovereignty is no longer glued to either of the elements of the triune principle and entities; at the utmost, it is tied to them but loosely and in portions much reduced in size and contents. The allegedly unbreakable marriage of power and politics is, however, ending in separation with a prospect of divorce.[3]

What seems problematic, instead, is the picture he draws of the new global stage:

> Sovereignty is nowadays, so to speak, unanchored and free-floating. Criteria of its allocation tend to be hotly contested, while the customary sequence of the principle of allocation and its application is in a great number of cases reversed. The principle tends to be retrospectively articulated in the aftermath of the allocating decision or deduced from the

---

2   Z. Bauman, "Times of interregnum", in *Ethics & Global Politics*, Vol. 5, No. 1, 2012, pp. 49-56. With regard to the political powerlessness of Europe, see also Étienne Balibar, "Interregnum", in Id., *Europe, crise et fin?*, Le Bord de l'eau, Lormont 2016, pp. 7-31.
3   Z. Bauman, op. cit., pp.49-50.

already accomplished state of affairs. Nation-states find themselves sharing the conflict-ridden and quarrelsome company of actual, aspiring or pretending, but always pugnaciously competitive sovereign subjects, with entities successfully evading the application of the heretofore binding triune principle of allocation, and all too often explicitly ignoring or stealthily sapping and impairing its designated objects.[4]

This intriguing scenario is in complete agreement with the image of "liquid modernity" that has made Bauman famous, but it is quite distant from all the various positions outlined in the present volume – starting from the position adopted by the present writer, who at the beginning of the new millennium, and hence even before Bauman, had actually proposed the term "interregnum" as a key to interpreting our present. In my book *The Passage West*, right from its first edition (2003), the reader will come across lines recalling "the current *interregnum* between the old inter-state framework and a new framework that has yet to be defined"[5]; or "this *time suspended* between the *no-longer* of the old inter-state order and the *not-yet* of a new supranational order"[6]; or passages which – as Bauman was later to do in his works – define the suspended

---

4   Ibid., p. 50.
5   G. Marramao, *The Passage West*, London-New York: Verso, 2012, p. 132 (original ed., *Passaggio a Occidente*, Bollati Boringhieri, Torino 2003). In the United States, The University of Michigan Library has devoted a volume to this book: "On Giacomo Marramao's 'The Passage West'", *Política Común*, Special Issue, Vol. 8, Michigan Publishing, Ann Arbor 2015 (It. transl., *Filosofia dei mondi globali. Conversazioni con Giacomo Marramao*, edited by Stefano Franchi and Manuela Marchesini, Bollati Boringhieri, Torino 2017 – contributions by Peter Baker, Martin Jay, Andy Lantz, Alberto Moreiras, Pedro Ángel Palou, Carlos Rodriguez, Teresa M. Vilarós, and Hayden White).
6   G. Marramao, *The Passage West*, cit. , p. 41. The full sentence reads as follows: "Due to the political void produced by the absence of global governance and of a legitimate institutional mediation (at this *time suspended* between the *no-longer* of the old inter-state order and the *not-yet* of a new supranational order), the sides of universalism and of differences stand in opposition, exacerbating their respective one-sidedness and hardening their position in the glocal pincer. The tension released from the *double bind* takes on the shape of a *conflict of identities* whose logic escapes the procedural *dispositifs* of control of contemporary 'polyarchies'."

time of the interregnum via the term interlude: "In this passage, European legal space risks situating itself in a no-man's-land, in a sort of *interlude* or time suspended between a 'democracy of identity' and a 'democracy of differences'. Despite Habermas' hopes, we are still far from a theory and a praxis able to legitimise itself through the 'inclusion of the Other'".[7]

Bauman appears to ignore, or to overlook, the retrieval of Carl Schmitt's concept of the Political and the redevelopments of the notion of the "state of exception" that have marked philosophical debate in Italy since the 1970s.[8] At the same time, he provides an all too linear picture of the dynamics of globalization, without grasping the copresence (and at times conflictual coexistence) within them of opposite tendencies: deterritorialization and reterritorialization, diffusion and concentration, interdependence and diaspora. This is why – like some of the authoritative authors featured in the present volume – I have stressed the need for a more rigorous lexicon and conceptual "toolbox", by suggesting we switch from deconstructive conformism to a reconstructive phase. In a book published in 2008 I wrote:

> If we truly wish to face the global risk lurking in the *current interregnum between the old Westphalian order and the new and still inceptive world order*, we must accomplish a drastic conversion from the deconstructive to the reconstructive phase. At a time in which deconstruction has become a kind of new conformism in all fields, it is necessary to reconstruct – which is to say, to conceptually *redefine* – the great plan of modern universalism, starting no longer from the *logic* of identity, but from the *criterion* of difference.[9]

---

7   Ibid., pp. 211-212.
8   In the academic year 1977-1978, I held a course on "The Concept of the Political in Carl Schmitt" at the University of Naples "L'Orientale", where I was teaching at the time (this was the first course on Schmitt held in an Italian university after WW2). I also took Schmitt as a term of comparison for "the Marxisms" of the interwar period in my book *Il Politico e le trasformazioni*, De Donato, Bari 1979.
9   G. Marramao, *La passione del presente*, Bollati Boringheri, Torino 2008, p. 42.

Diaspora e interregno is the title of a section of the same book devoted to the fate of law in a "post-Hobbesian order" (to use what has become a classic expression by Philippe Schmitter).[10]

The construction of a new concept of the Political capable of going beyond Carl Schmitt and Antonio Gramsci – the two theorists who, from opposite sides, had best grasped the change in form that politics was undergoing well into the 20th century – must place three fundamental aspects at the centre of its analysis today.

First of all: the epistemological turn brought about by the emergence of political economy. Marx – the mature Marx of the *Grundrisse* and *Capital* – had perfectly grasped the sharply innovative character of that new science which combined into an oxymoron two terms which the Classical tradition had kept separate: the *oikos*, the domestic sphere of material production-reproduction; and the *polis*, the sphere of politics as the *praxis* of public governance. From Adam Smith onwards, the aim and source of the State's legitimacy was no longer the "good life", but the "wealth of the Nation". Smith paid close attention to the interconnection between economics, politics, and law, aware of the fact that the market's "invisible hand" needs the State's "visible hand" in order to function.

Secondly, the coexistence of two principles in the five "long centuries" of modernity: the principle of "globality" and that of "territoriality". These themes occur in the works of Giovanni Arrighi, an economic sociologist with an eye for history,[11] and of Charles Maier, a historian who pays close attention to the political and social sciences.[12] The former has provided a crucial contribution to the analysis of the globalised world, not least from a comparative perspective. The latter has brought into focus the features of "Leviathan 2.0", i.e. the form of State that established

---

10 Cf. ibid., pp. 181 ff.
11 *The Long Twentieth Century: Money, Power, and the Origins of Our Times*, new edition, London-New York: Verso, 2009.
12 Ch. S. Maier, *Leviathan 2.0: Inventing Modern Statehood*, The President and Fellows of Harvard College, Cambridge, MA 2012; *Once Within Borders:. Territories of Power, Wealth and Belonging since 1500*, The President and Fellows of Harvard College, Cambridge, MA 2016.

itself between the mid-19th and mid-20th centuries, suggesting that one of the paradoxical effects of the digital age has been the decline of the paradigm of governance through the establishment of a "Leviathan 3.0" and a return to the logic of territorial boundaries. *Thirdly*, the non-interchangeability of the concepts of "capital" and "capitalism". As I have already argued in my book *Dopo il Leviatano*, "the dominance of global capital does not give rise to a single, standardised version of capitalism (a term which is actually foreign to the Marxian vocabulary and which only attained a scientific standing with Sombart and Weber), but rather to a multiplicity of 'capitalisms'".[13] These "capitalisms" – and we here get to the crucial point – differ not only from an ethnic-cultural perspective, but also and especially from a political standpoint.

In the age of global hyper-modernity, we thus witness the reproduction of the form of "political capitalism" which Max Weber had envisaged in §31 of *Wirtschaft und Gesellschaft*, where he had presented it as an anomalous iteration, compared to the rationality of modern Western capitalism. This anomaly outlines a new global world that is far from "liquid", a world dominated by an antagonistic duumvirate of political capitalisms – the United States and China – that encapsulate the economic, commercial, and technological dynamics within a logic and strategy of power.[14]

This new bipolar version of what Weber calls *politischer Kapitalismus* would not appear to bode well for the future of the planet and its peoples. It is already creating a series of conflictual fault lines: from the fault line of inequality, which is now progressively impoverishing the middle classes in developed countries, to the identitarian conflicts between territorial nationalities and trans-territorial diasporic communities. This perennial instability has given rise to a post-hegemonic configuration of the world, marked by a crisis of authority on a global scale. This crisis brings into play the problem of a *horizontal reconstruction of the Political*

---

13 G. Marramao, *Dopo il Leviatano*, new ed., Bollati Boringhieri, Torino 2013, pp. 463-464.
14 On this topic, see the recent volume by A. Aresu, *Le potenze del capitalismo politico: Stati Uniti e Cina*, La Nave di Teseo, Milano 2020.

hinging on the web of subjectivities and individual differences. The contributions featured in the present volume focus precisely on such topics: the relation (and possible transition) between biopolitics and post-hegemony; the genealogy of the subject; the redefinition of the concept of community; and the multitude-people hendiadys.

The populist syndrome is at once a symptom and a constitutive factor of this crisis of authority. In its twofold form as political populism and digital-media-videocratic neopopulism, the populist phenomenon represents a problem that is wholly *internal* to the dynamics of the transformation of democracy.[15] This is a problem that can be traced back to the very origins of Western democracy: like all foundational terms, the word "people" is subject to that indeterminacy principle that makes it the underlying energy and legitimising power of democracy. Yet the people is not merely a concept or a subject – both of which, by definition, are nowhere to be found. The people is also a people-event: a driving force of history.

This leads us to the threshold of the "other stage" of our introductory essay. And, as we shall see, on this new stage of the interregnum, the first pillar of the Political to be put under stress will be precisely the Weberian paradigm of the legitimation of power.

However, in writing about Weber on the centenary of his death, we should always remember – which is to say, always cherish in our hearts and minds – the closing words of the "Politik als Beruf" lecture, with which this great theoretician of "disenchantment", instead of reducing politics to the art of what is possible, placed it in direct relation to the *impossible*:

> Politics is a strong and slow boring of hard boards. It takes both passion and perspective. Certainly all historical experience confirms the truth --that man would not have attained the possible unless time and again he had reached out for the impossible.[16]

---

15 See P. Rosanvallon, 'Penser le populisme', in *La vie des idées*, 27 September 2011. Even Umberto Coldagelli – a notable historian and intellectual belonging to the Italian "workerist" tradition – has highlighted the "populist" features of the presidentialism of the Fifth Republic: see U. Coldagelli, *La quinta repubblica da De Gaulle a Sarkozy*, Donzelli, Roma 2009.
16 M. Weber, "Politik als Beruf" (1918), in *Gesammelte politische Schriften*, Duncker & Humblot, Munich 1921, p. 450; English

The Other Scene
On the Populist Syndrome. Delegitimization as a Political strategy

1. From legitimate power to delegitimized power

The tradition of social thought that, from Max Weber onwards, has established the problem of legitimation at the centre of the analysis of power is now facing serious difficulties owing to the paradoxical transformation which has occurred in the logic of democratic systems. Political conflict appears to be increasingly polarized through the opposite tendency towards delegitimization. Parties, movements, and agencies competing for the acquisition of power seem to no longer be directing their action towards legitimizing their own ideas and programmes, but rather towards the delegitimization of their opponents. A radical or even antagonistic kind of competition based on mutual recognition between competing factions has increasingly come to be replaced by the disavowal and disrepute of the opponent as a privileged means of acquiring the sort of "political surplus value" capable of ensuring stable popular consensus.

The thesis I wish to submit is that the shifting of the centre of gravity in democratic competition from the problem of legitimization to the strategy of delegitimization represents the common denominator among the many variants of the phenomenon referred to by vague terms such as "populism", "national-populism", and "sovereignism". Following the transition from the democracy of parties to the "democracy of the public"[17] – marked by the decline of the political cultures of the post-WWII period, by the destructuring of mass parties, and by a twofold process of personalization and mediatization – the phenomenon in question has spelled the dawn of a new era for democratic dynamics. This era is characterised by what I would define as the "populist

---

translation, "Politics as a Vocation", in M. Weber, *Essays in Sociology*, trans. and ed. by H.H. Gerth and C. Wright Mills, New York: Oxford University Press, 1946, p. 128.

17 As is widely known, the expression was first formulated by Bernard Manin, *Principes du gouvernement représentatif*, Calmann-Lévy, Paris 1995.

syndrome", something which Ilvo Diamanti and Marc Lazar have instead described using the memorable term "popolocrazia" ("people-cracy").[18] Through their delegitimizing aggressiveness and "rejection of any sort of politics", populist movements today represent "the manifestation of a democratic problem", while at the same time standing as the "expression of and means towards what are perhaps crucial metamorphoses of our democracies".[19]

But here a first problem emerges: to what extent does the common denominator of delegitimization mark a truly new phenomenon, as opposed to the re-emergence – in other forms and in a different historical context – of what has been a constitutive factor of Western democracy from its very origins? Addressing a key issue such as that of delegitimization in an eminently comparative historical and linguistic – rather than merely political – context calls for a preliminary word of caution.

Clearly, this is a burning issue: the cross-sectional nature of "delegitimizing rhetoric" in the various European political systems (and, to an almost grotesque level, in US democracy) is such a manifest phenomenon that one does not need particularly sophisticated analytical tools to detect it. However, it is only possible to grasp its actual impact by viewing the present from a distance through the use of what Carlo Ginzburg would call an "inverted telescope".

Only by adopting this reverse perspective is it possible to grasp that *untimely fold of the present* capable of bringing out enduring features and changes, forms of continuity and breaks, the past of what is new and the memory of the future. Delegitimization – a term coined in relatively recent times, but which has spread to almost all Western languages – designates a "characteristic aspect of the contemporary political sphere" and a "symbolic-discursive mode of political propaganda", as historian Fulvio Cammarano has shown. However, delegitimization practices have de facto been at work from the very start in this field, which in Classical Greece was defined – according to Christian Meier's famous reconstruction[20]

---

18 I. Diamanti-M. Lazar, *Popolocrazia. La metamorfosi delle nostre democrazie*, Laterza, Roma-Bari 2018.
19 Ibid., p. 7.
20 *Die Entstehung des Politischen bei den Griechen*, Suhrkamp, Frankfurt am Main 1980.

– using a substantivized adjective that was destined to emerge as one of the central categories in our vocabulary: *politics*.

2. Delegitimization and state of exception

Since, for obvious reasons, this is not the place where to newly present the kind of genealogical reconstructions I have offered elsewhere,[21] I will limit myself to a few observations. Their aim will be to highlight the logically asymmetrical and historically discontinuous relationship between the pairs of terms legitimacy/illegitimacy and legitimization/delegitimization: the former constituted by a vertical axiality of a structural-regulatory sort, the other by a horizontal axiality of the historical-dynamic sort.

Very succinctly: the use of the non-*legitimus* argument as a strategic weapon to devalue political opponents marks the whole history of political theory and praxis in the West, starting from the development of the concept of the "political" in Greece through the distinction between what is in compliance with the *koinonia*, the shared space of the *polis*, and what is not. The etymology of *legitimus*, like the Greek term *nomimon*, suggests a relationship based on compliance with the law. But the law in question here is originally *Nomos*: the supreme ordering principle – *Nomos basileus*, as illustrated by Marcello Gigante[22] and later, in the footsteps of Carl Schmitt, by Pier Paolo Portinaro[23] – that is irreducible to the positive law established by *kratos*, yet shaped and permeated by justice. Therefore, all real *nomimon* is also *dikaion*.

We thus witness the emergence of a recurrent ethical feature which – periodical turns and breaks notwithstanding – runs through all the various stages of ancient and medieval natural law, down to contractualism and modern constitutionalism. Here the fundamental principles of the Constitution receive a legitimizing/

---

21   I am referring, in particular, to *The Passage West: Philosophy After the Age of the Nation State*, Verso, London-New York 2012.
22   See M. Gigante, *Nomos Basileus*, Edizioni Glaux, Napoli 1956 (new ed., Bibliopolis, Napoli 1993).
23   See P.P. Portinaro, *Appropriazione, distribuzione, produzione. Materiali per una teoria del "nomos"*, Angeli, Milano 1983; Id., *Il realismo politico*, Laterza, Roma-Bari 1999.

delegitimizing *potestas*, an inclusive/exclusive power, as a *trait d'union* between law and politics (or, better, between the regulatory axioms of law and the informative principles of politics). However, in the natural law tradition itself, the question of legitimacy acquires a crucial role: in the form of a circle between the validity and the effectiveness of the legal system (Hans Kelsen), as the simultaneously effective and symbolic surplus value of charisma (Max Weber), or through a reference to the "state of exception" as a "force of law" that is extra-legal (yet not extra-juridical, i.e. which cannot be confused with mere force) and which at its core carries a legitimacy that exceeds legality (Carl Schmitt). Schmitt's famous formula "Sovereign is he who decides the state of exception" would thus come to mean: "Sovereign is he who decides on legitimacy", i.e. "Sovereign is he who has the power to legitimately proclaim the suspension of the law".

Hence the crucial question: on the basis of what criterion can we define the dimension and subject of legitimacy? Schmitt identifies this criterion in the constitutive antithesis of the Political: the dividing line between friend and enemy. Only he who is capable of tracing this line has the legitimacy to proclaim the state of exception. Yet this does not at all delegitimize one's enemy (understood as *hostis*, or public enemy, as opposed to *inimicus*, or private enemy): in fact, he receives full acknowledgement as a legitimate opponent. On the other hand, Weber identifies the common denominator of the three ideal forms of legitimate power (traditional, rational-legal, and charismatic) – which are only distinguishable on the epistemic level, whereas in practice they are intertwined – in the *belief* of "the governed". However, it must be noted that, from Weber's perspective, "belief in legitimacy" constitutes not an *effect* but a *source* of power (hence the radical difference between his view and Foucault's, for instance).

3. *From pluralism to the polytheism of values*

In accordance with the paradigmatic assumption of legal positivism, the surplus or tension between legitimacy and legality still falls within a vertical kind of axiality centred on the relation between those who govern and those who are governed. Not least for this reason, as the analysis formulated by Guglielmo Ferrero many years ago suggests,[24] the transition to democratic legitimacy is destined to prove difficult. However, despite the endurance of motifs that flow throughout the history of Western politics as an underground current, the issues at stake change considerably once we pass from the vertical axiality of legitimate-illegitimate to the horizontal one of legitimization-delegitimization as a *process*.

As Reinhart Koselleck has shown in his studies on the transformation of the socio-political lexicon in the modern age,[25] the turning point at which the new constellation of the dynamic terms of modernity emerged (from the neologism *Weltgeschichte*, "Universal history" or "World-history", to the semantic redefinition of terms such as progress, revolution, and liberation) must be placed between the mid-18th and the mid-19th century. In this period of crucial transformations we witness the emergence of new pairs of opposites (to mention only the most influential: revolution-reaction, progress-conservation, right-left, nationalism-cosmopolitanism) that fostered incompatible worldviews. Their tendency towards mutual delegitimization gives rise to a horizontal axiality which is exactly the reverse of the horizontalness of the pact: the axiality of the conflict of values.

From being an assumption, legitimization is thus turned into an objective or thing at stake. It no longer coincides – as in Weber's famous threefold division of forms of legitimate power – with conformity to tradition (to the authority of the "eternal yesterday"), commitment to the charismatic power of a leader or movement, or reliance on the "power of the law", but rather with a rhetorical-strategic device for devaluation. Nevertheless,

---

24 See G. Ferrero, *Potere. I geni invisibili della Città*, SugarCo, Milano 1981.
25 See R. Koselleck, *Zeitschichten. Studien zur Historik*, Suhrkamp, Frankfurt am Main 2000. I have engaged in an extended intellectual dialogue with Koselleck, as witnessed by my books *Potere e secolarizzazione* (1983), new and expanded ed., Bollati Boringhieri, Torino 2005; *La passione del presente. Breve lessico della modernità-mondo*, Bollati Boringhieri, Torino 2008; and *Dopo il Leviatano. Individuo e comunità* (1990), third, expanded ed., Bollati Boringhieri, Torino 2013.

the scenario of a "polytheism of values" now comes across as a genuine prophecy in the face of the conflicts over identity that are tearing Europe and the whole globalized world apart. This is only the case, however, if this scenario is not mistaken for an edifying praise of the pluralism and ethical relativism of points of view (*Standpunkte*), but is grasped in terms of a tragic exclusiveness of points of attack (*Angriffspunkte*) engaged in a fatal dispute. In this case too, however, it is a matter of distinguishing between a conflict of values which Schmitt himself regarded as worse and deadlier than Hobbes' *bellum omnium contra omnes* and the strategies of mutual delegitimization adopted by political rivals pursuing objectives pertaining to the seizing of power.

4. The People and its double

The delegitimization practices characterizing democratic societies fall along a shadow line, a boundary between law, politics, and morality: a hybrid symbolic space, steeped in ideological influences, summary narratives, and a rhetoric of discredit which, through the new media, use history as a means of self-legitimization, with selective or sometimes arbitrary flippancy. In the metamorphoses which have affected the public sphere, the legitimization/delegitimization antithesis thus implies a web-like system of references between discursive practices, strategic logics, and identitarian dynamics.

The effects of political communication are not merely cognitive, as they also affect the performative power of words across different pragmatic-linguistic contexts. The adoption of a perspective centred on the intertwining of historical semantics, linguistics, and cultural analysis not only makes it possible to bring into focus the systemic nature of contrastive identity – to consider the case of Italy – but opens up the path to a medium/long-term reconstruction of the "divisiveness" which marks the country's political history. The rift in question does not concern only its republican phase – through the well-known phenomenon of *conventio ad excludendum*, a legacy of the "long civil war of the 20th century" – but can be traced back to the very origins of the process of Italian political unification.

Indeed, the theme of "two nations" or "two peoples" was put forward as early as 1868 by Angelo Camillo De Meis in his essay "Il Sovrano", republished by Benedetto Croce in 1927, along with a polemic against Carducci and Fiorentino: "As long as modern society is divided into two peoples" – De Meis wrote – "a middle ground will always be necessary where they can meet and reach some mutual understanding [...]. In Italy the two modern Peoples are deeply separated; more than elsewhere, perhaps, because it is the centre and headquarters of the religion of Celtic-Latin Europe. They cannot understand each other, and they are naturally divided into two opposite and enemy camps. Therefore, no real and perfect Sovereignty is possible, but only Tyranny."[26]

We shall soon turn to consider the significance of these observations for the issue of memory and its multidimensionality. First, though, there is a question we must address.

5. Community and the citizenship gap

Delegitimization is no doubt a recurrent feature of political conflict: we need only consider Machiavelli's "iniurie" ("injuries"). But precisely for this reason, just like conflict *sans phrase*, it risks proving an empty vessel. It can only produce effects in terms of knowledge if it is set in relation to specific contexts and contents. Today political conflict appears to be permeated by ethical, religious, and anthropological elements: far from being accessory, the elements are constitutive of identitarian logics that have taken the place of the ideological frameworks known (and experienced) over the last two years of modernity. These have been long centuries: the 20th century too was not a short one – indeed, Giovanni Arrighi has rightly referred to it as "the long 20th century".

At the turn of the 21st century, we have witnessed the failure of the two primary models of citizenship integration theorized and practised over the course of modernity: the universalist-assimilationist republican model and the strong differentialist-multiculturalist model – what Seyla Benhabib has described as

---

26 A.C. De Meis, *Il Sovrano. Saggio di Filosofia politica con riferenza all'Italia*, ed. by Benedetto Croce, Laterza, Bari 1927, pp. 13-14.

the "mosaic" model. It is an irony of history that the "République model" and the "Londonistan model" give rise to the same forms of identitarian conflict, marked by the transition from the logic of the rational assessment of one's interests to the logic of belonging (or of "conversion", to borrow Alessandro Pizzorno's term).[27] To complicate matters, the globalized world finds itself in a sort of 'interregnum' between the 'no longer' of the old order based on sovereign nation-states and the 'not yet' of a post-national order which, after having struggled to take shape, now appears to be caving in upon itself, by raising anachronistic borders and coagulating into a geopolitics and geoeconomics of large spaces dominated by continent-states: from the United States to China, and from India to Russia and Brazil. In this interregnum, as in all interregnums, monstrous hybrids are already coming to light that might spell the end of that complex of knowledge and practices which for the past 2,500 years we have called politics.

One of these hybrids is that mix of "anti-politics" (a misleading polemical term used to describe anti-establishment movements) and hyper-democratic rhetoric that characterises the double nature of the People in populist movements. The People presents itself, on the one hand, as a homogeneous and identity-shaping entity and, on the other, as "the virtuous people against its corrupt representatives", whose sovereignty can only be reaffirmed by a leader capable of embodying its will.[28]

However, there is also a theoretically more sophisticated version of populism which is largely overlooked by mainstream political science. It stands in open contrast to the 'anti-political' and delegitimizing tendency, and hedges its bets on the "populist moment" as the only possible means of ensuring the "return of the Political" from the perspective of a radical democracy, yet not an "immediate democracy"[29] – an antagonistic yet at the same time

---

27 See the crucial collection of essays *Il velo della diversità. Studi su razionalità e riconoscimento*, Feltrinelli, Milano 2007.
28 See I. Diamanti-M. Lazar, *Popolocrazia*, cit., p. 8.
29 Condorcet uses this expression in the pamphlet *Aux amis de la liberté sur les moyens d'en assurer la durée* (1790), in Œuvres de Condorcet, t. X, Paris 1847, pp. 178-179.

pluralistic and anti-authoritarian democracy. Without engaging with this theoretically strong proposal, any attempt to make sense of the populist syndrome is bound to be purely illusionary.

6. Political populism

When I speak of the theoretically strong proposal of a *political populism*, what I am referring to in particular is the work carried out by Ernesto Laclau in the philosophical field and by Chantal Mouffe in that of political science. To speak of the personality, philosophical work, passion, and political commitment of Ernesto Laclau today is difficult for anyone, given the complexity and relevance of his work.[30] But it is a particularly painful task for someone like the present writer, who was a friend of Laclau's and engaged with him, at different stages, across the two shores of the Atlantic from the late 1970s onwards. I can never forget our last meeting in Paris in December 2013, when the two of us served on the search committee for a post at the Sorbonne, together with Myriam Revault d'Allonnes, Pierre Rosanvallon, and other colleagues. Nor can I forget the lengthy email he sent me the day before his unexpected death in Seville on 13 April 2014, when he was taking part in a conference I too had meant to attend – having been forced to change my plans at the last minute. His remarkable contribution to the philosophical and political understanding of our times has been a focus of international debate for decades, following the publication of his famous 1985 book *Hegemony and Socialist Strategy*, co-authored by Chantal Mouffe; the 1996 essay *Emancipation(s)*; and the 2000 volume *Contingency, Hegemony, Universality* (written in collaboration with Judith Butler and Slavoj Žižek). It has acquired particular relevance with his 2005 book *On Populist Reason*. (In this context, however, we should not overlook Chantal Mouffe's contribution to the recovery, extension, and redefinition of Carl Schmitt's "concept of the Political" in recent

---

30 I here draw upon some of the ideas I developed in the essay *Conflicto, populismo, hegemonía*, in "Debates y Combates", a. 5 (2015), Edición Homenaje. Ernesto Laclau, Vol. 2, pp. 63-70.

years: from the 2005 essay *On the Political* to the 2018 volume *For a Left Populism*).

At a lecture given in Rome not long before his death, Laclau offered – in the clear and succinct form typical of oral presentations – a sort of "secular arm" or *in actu* political translation of his main theoretical statements.[31] These statements revolve around the key notions of conflict, populism, and hegemony, and their radical redefinition from a discursive and – crucially, for this is where the theoretical core of his proposal lies – *anti-essentialistic* perspective. Without clearly grasping this assumption, namely Laclau's radical criticism of all forms of metaphysical substantialism or essentialism, it is impossible to understand the strictly *political* characterization of his notion of populism: a notion which conflicts with anti-political versions of populism that postulate the subject-people as an entity which is already a given, already constituted.

On various occasions Laclau had stressed how the "social" presents itself with a marked degree of complexity and heterogeneity in contemporary societies. This does not imply the disappearance of the conflict between capital and labour that lies at the centre of the classic Marxian analysis of the capitalist mode of production. However, it requires its redefinition and re-contextualization in relation to the "emergence of equally radical conflicts, such as the environmental, over common resources such as water, and frequent revolts against exclusion and social marginalization on a planetary scale." The problem which emerges, then, is "the political articulation of these conflicts": to think of politics is to think of a "hegemonic practice" capable of recomposing into a unitary strategy a range of differences, conflicting polarities, and variety of demands that would otherwise be dispersed.

This theoretical plan for a recovery and overall reformulation of the Gramscian concept of hegemony – carried forth by Laclau through his close intellectual partnership with Chantal Mouffe, whose reflections on the "Political", as already stressed, represent an original contribution and crucial complement to Laclau's own work – was presented as "post-Marxist" from as early as 1985:

---

31   See E. Laclau, *Conflitto, populismo, egemonia*, foreword by Giacomo Marramao, in "Parolechiave", no. 52, 2014, pp. 67-74.

with the publication, before the fall of the Berlin Wall, of their work *Hegemony and Socialist Strategy*. In this important book (which had a considerable influence on the international debate in the field), the theory of hegemony which Gramsci developed in his *Prison Notebooks* is, on the one hand, envisaged as the turning point for a break with Marx's "economicism" and for a profound reassessment of the Leninist conception of politics. On the other hand, it is taken as a point of departure to be reformulated in terms of "discourse theory".

The reformulation of the concept of hegemony suggested by Laclau (and Mouffe) is achieved through a skilful combinatory logic, capable of combining and crossing – not without certain unresolved issues and internal tensions – five different theoretical coordinates: Saussure's linguistics, Lacanian psychoanalysis, the Gramscian legacy filtered through Althusser's *coupure épistémologique*, post-structuralism (in Derrida's, rather than Foucault's, version), and the cultural turn (adopted, with substantial changes, in Stuart Hall's version, starting from the second stage of British Cultural Studies and Postcolonial Studies). The outcome of this *ars combinatoria* is the tracing of the classic hendiadys economy/society, community/culture, and politics/hegemony back to Discourse Theory.

7. Anti-essentialism: the People as a political construction

"Discourse" is therefore the keyword in Laclau's theoretical programme: an *anti-essentialistic* assumption which dissolves all pre-established centrality, establishing political subjectivity within a hegemonic game based on a logic of inclusion/exclusion, openness/closure. The departure from the foundationalist perspective (even in its Marxist variants) has one crucial consequence, which is often overlooked by critics operating within mainstream political science. The Subject neither precedes nor establishes the discourse but, on the contrary, is the product of a "subjectivization" process brought about by the discourse itself: more precisely – and more in keeping with Laclau's language – by discursive practices. In other words, originally there is no Subject, but only a Relation, understood not as "the name of a *given* relational concept",[32] but as a constellation of actions and relational practices that always make the subjects. Within this constellation – the primary setting for society – there are no substantial identities (be they of an individualistic or community sort), but only conflicting polycentric dynamics between irreducible *differences*. Hence the reason why, again in keeping with the anti-essentialistic assumption, just as there are no pre-established individual subjects (as conceived in modern contractualism, from Hobbes onwards), according to Laclau there cannot be any "society" as a presupposed totality or spontaneous pullulation (in Durkheim's sense or in that of the various forms of holism, from Aristotle to contemporary communitarians).

For Laclau, as much as for Cornelius Castoriadis, society does not exist except as an "imaginary institution". What sociologists and cultural anthropologists call the "social bond" is actually the contingent result of discursive practices whose logic always coincides with a strategy aimed at domination. The notion of "discourse", then, far from ultimately amounting to a linguistic-communicative modality, indicates the construction of a relational context of meaning whose shifting epicentre – what is at stake – is represented by the question of power.

Here we find another crucial step in Laclau's theory: just as, based on such promises, it has become meaningless to distinguish between logic and strategy (since power is not a superstructure but a constitutive factor within language itself), so the Foucaultian distinction between discursive and non-discursive practices, "words" and "things", language and praxis, loses all meaning.

Right from its grammatical and syntactical structure, the order of the discourse presents itself as an *inextricable web between material dimension and symbolic sphere*. From this perspective, not only the social structure but the "economy" itself, released from its fetishised objectivity, presents itself as a complex articulation of relational and practical-discursive differences. In one respect, this aspect was already foreshadowed by Marx through the notion of "relations of production"; in another respect, it has

---

[32] E. Laclau-C. Mouffe, *Hegemony and Socialist Strategy: Towards a Radical Democratic Politics*, Verso, London 1985, p. 93.

become crystallised into what is still a classic treatment, revolving around the distinction between basic structure and superstructure. Discourse theory, which is played out in the pair of terms signifier/signified, resolves the aporia inherent in the Marxian topic, insofar as the symbolic dimension of "meaning" and "culture" is removed from the superstructural level and grafted upon the fabric of the constitutive practices of "material" relations themselves.

But – and the weight of this *but* cannot be overstated, for without it we would risk trivializing Laclau's position almost to the point of making a caricature of it – there is no discursive context capable of standing as a saturated totality in which the "sign" is realised in the "meaning", in which signifiers resolve all possible meanings within themselves. Herein lies the crucial function exercised within Laclau's reflection by a particularly sophisticated and conceptually challenging leitmotiv, which I can only briefly outline here: the them of the "empty signifier". The constitutively partial character of an "order of discourse" whose logic is always strategically oriented imposes the ineluctable destiny of partiality and contingency on that order.

Only in the light of these premises is it possible to understand what might at first sight seem like a provocative statement by Laclau, who affirms the perfect coincidence between populism and politics (this statement already occurs in the final chapter of his first work, *Politics and Ideology in Marxist Theory: Capitalism-Fascism-Populism*, published in 1977; and it is further developed in the first chapter of *Hegemony and Socialist Strategy*). Just like discourse, the signifier People presents itself as something akin to what mathematicians call an "unsaturated formula": a signifier liable to acquire different meanings, depending on the context, but never to realize all its possible meanings in itself. However, the emptier this signifier is, the more it must logically and strategically present itself as a totality. For this simple yet decisive reason, the hidden meaning of the People as a political construct must always be discovered in its implicit – i.e. (in Freudian terms of *Verdrängung* and *Verwerfung*) repressed, yet precisely for this reason constitutive – reference to a "reject", an excluded remainder: women, slaves, and foreigners with respect to the Greek *demos*, the *plebs* with respect to the Roman *populus*.

Besides, gazing back at the oldest democracy of modernity, who could ever deny the non-descriptive but performative character of the formula *"We, the People"*?

Moving on from theoretical statements to more strictly political ones, Laclau's aim is to bind together populism and radical democracy, based on a hegemonic strategy designed to cross the boundary that separates the people from its remainder, by translating the logic of difference (the sum of dispersed demands addressed to power) into a "logic of equivalence" that aligns these claims around an "empty signifier". Laclau is lucidly aware that even the most democratically inclusive operation will nonetheless produce a remainder: a marker of the contingency of all hegemonic practices and, at the same time, a guarantee of the opening up of conflicts and dynamics of change. A work of translation of this sort can never lead to the solving or neutralizing of conflict; rather, it always implies the construction of an antagonistic boundary between the "people" and the authorities.

"Radical politics for me means the political construction of the people", Laclau repeatedly stated. Yet the political construction of the people occurs inside and outside the State simultaneously: inside the State, as the conflict over the acknowledgement of particular interests; outside the State, as it "challenges the monopoly of political decision-making". For this reason, *populist politics should not be mistaken for a form of "plebiscitarianism"*; on the contrary, it postulates a dynamic intertwining between direct and representative democracy. And it is precisely this intertwining that Laclau describes through the challenging expression "radical democracy".

A few more words to wrap up this whole issue. It has often been stressed that the populistic idea of Nation carries considerable risks in terms of abuse of power, intolerance, and the curtailment of liberty. Such concerns are far from ill-founded. However, Laclau has often responded by stressing how, in Western democratic systems, the rhetoric centred on "empty signifiers" such as Freedom, Civilization, and Justice in turn corresponds to a political-discursive strategy which, while on the surface asserting universality, actually engenders specific forms of discrimination and marginalisation. The real risk in Laclau's theory of populism

– a risk which critics have often overlooked – is instead of a radically opposite nature: it concerns the fragility of the project of the recomposition of differences that, within the new global constellation (however we wish to interpret or represent it), hardly seem to fit with an idea of people and politics confined to the national paradigm.

I shall leave aside here the reservations of those people who, like the present writer, do not identify with "populist reason", yet feel the need to stress the *cognitive dissonance* engendered by the divergent use of the term "populism", or even "homeland", in Europe and Latin America by distinguishing between Latin-American political populism and the xenophobic, media-driven neo-populism of Europe. However, we still need to consider the theoretical complexity and seriousness of the problem raised by Ernesto Laclau.

The anti-essentialistic perspective of his theoretical programme readily embraces the *pars destruens* of that great tradition in European thought which, from Hobbes to Kelsen (but also from Weber to Luhmann and Habermas himself), denies the People any real existence, taking instead a multitude of singularities and differences as its starting point. But whereas, in their *pars construens*, both Hobbes and Kelsen infer from this premise that the people is a juridical construct produced by the neutral device of sovereignty and/or that of the positive system of laws, the People represents a *political construct*: a construct without which the life and efficacy of the juridical order would lose all meaning.

How can we deny, then, the untimely timeliness of this message? Still...

8. *Power without authority: the double regime of memory*

Still, a lot remains to be discussed, revised, and challenged.

First of all, there is the question of the double soul of modern democracy:

(a) the "Madisonian" soul, with its principle of the limitation of power, including the power of the "sovereign people";

(b) the "populist" soul, with the principle of participation.

This constitutive duplicity gives rise to the "perennial tension within Western constitutionalism between *juridical limitation* and *political responsibility*" and, with it, the risk of two involutional tendencies: democracy without rights and rights without democracy.[33]

Second, there is the radical difference between Laclau and Mouffe's passionately political and engaging populism and the *media-driven neo-populism* of our digitalised societies. In the latter case, we find not a construction of the idea of a people, but its deconstruction and de-structuring into a mass of isolated individuals reduced to a mere audience, despite the illusion that it is possible for them to acquire a leading role through the Web. It is like a neo-Baroque spectatorial syndrome: *Spectator sum in hac scena, non actor*....

Therefore, in the so-called "digital populism" of today – with its strategies of discredit and casual use of fake news, and "formatted" states of exception, artfully constructed according to an "occasionalism" that is light-years away from the great, tragic politics of the 20th century – it is easy to see the other side of the neo-liberal breakdown of community bonds.

What destiny, then, awaits democratic polyarchies? There is only one way to attempt to regenerate democracy: by moving away from the language of legitimation/delegitimization for good, in order to recover the theme of authority.

This recovery, however, must coincide with a radical redefinition of the concept.[34] In the current interregnum, marked by *power without authority* and by *authority devoid of power*, it is necessary to sever the bond which keeps the idea of authority anchored in the *arché*, in the Principate-Principle, and to envisage it instead as an *auctoritas* understood – according to its etymology – as an *augere*,

---

33 See F. Raniolo, *Democrazie sotto stress e tendenze illiberali*, in "Paradoxa", a. XIII, no. 3, July-September 2019, p. 52.
34 For a recovery and redefinition of the theme of authority, in opposition to the logic of power, I will refer to the remarks I have put forward in *Against Power: For an Overhaul of Crtical Theory*, Rowman and Littlefield, Lanham, MD 2016, following a theoretical path that is in many respects close to the "philosophy of difference": see esp. Luisa Muraro, *Autorità*, Rosenberg & Sellier, Torino 2013.

an *augmentum*, a symbolic growth and energy autonomously stemming from the dynamics of cooperation and conflict within the body politic. In other words, it is a matter of rethinking the Machiavellian motif of a generative, free, and cohesive republic, capable of forming a horizon of meaning for individual and collective action.

However, by now shifting our focus to the nexus between philosophy, politics, and history, we must envisage a process of constituting subjectivities capable – in the wake of the significant distinction introduced by Aleida Assmann[35] – of linking two different dimensions of memory:

(a) *function-memory*, in its twofold character: *selective*, insofar as it transmits foundational identity values, and *constructive* of a horizon of meaning for the community;

(b) *storage-memory*, which preserves the non-functional, the excluded, the "surpassed", and – with it – "the repository of lost opportunities", the alternatives excluded and defeated by individual and collective history, or unrealised, "submerged", and latent possibilities.

Within the context of this layered vision of historical time, there is also an urgent need to rethink the time of politics and of its fields of action, beyond the classic antithesis between line and circle, cyclical and linear time.

By setting out from this, a counter-strategy must be developed capable of slowing down and inverting a drift of democracy, which today appears to be increasingly marked by the populist syndrome.

---

35 See A. Assmann, *Ricordare. Forme e mutamenti della memoria culturale*, Bologna, Il Mulino, 2002.

SECTION 1

THE LONG SHADOW OF LEVIATHAN

Gareth Williams

IN THE WAKE OF LEVIATHAN
From Biopolitics to Posthegemony

It is widely recognized that Michel Foucault's approach to and exploration of biopolitics was an attempt to register and explain the historical shift in sovereign power from the traditional Hobbesian right to take life or let live to the modern right to make live and let die (2003, pp. 240-241). In Foucault's accounts in *Society Must Be Defended* and *The Birth of Biopolitics* (2008) the emergence of modern biopolitical power resulted from the advent of a modern bourgeois political economy extended in conjunction with the liberal rationalization and regularization of the population in its entirety as an inherently political and biological affair rooted in the question of mortality, via, for example, the study and amelioration of the ratio of births to deaths, of the rate of reproduction, of the fertility of a population, of public hygiene, insurance, safety measures, savings etc. In Foucault's lectures biopolitics is the work neither "of the" political state nor "of" civil society alone, but the calculative demand for an increasingly technologically driven regime of production capable of containing both subject and object, extending the efficient enhancement of value extraction on both sides of the production equation («Production produces not only an object for the subject but also a subject for the object», Marx had indicated in the *Grundrisse,* 1993, p. 92). Biopolitics is in this sense the regularizing work of a bourgeois economic expansion that traverses and supersedes both the political state and civil society "in the name of" an expanded conceptualization and understanding of sovereign power, in particular its calculated individualization and collectivization of the question of the "life" of the modern subject. The ontological question of death, on the other hand, remained veiled and undefined in the bourgeois anthropologization, or bio-politicization, of the living. I will return to this question below.

In *The Prison Notebooks* penned between 1929 and 1935, Antonio Gramsci formulated state hegemony as «the entire complex of practical and theoretical activities with which the ruling class not only justifies and maintains its dominance, but manages to win the active consent of those over whom it rules» (1971, p. 244). Hegemony in Gramsci was mobilized to address the bourgeois seizure of power as the institutional forging of mediated subordination and consent from within the passive revolution of the Risorgimento and the emergent integral state. Foucault's use of biopolitics, it could be said, explains the passiveness of a passive revolution in the wake or in the absence of Jacobinist violence. In this context, biopolitics produces the full socialization of consent and consensus by installing the regularization of the life-death relation at the heart of the social via a bourgeois economic sphere built on the calculations and reproduction of *ratio*. From a purely Gramscian perspective biopolitics underpins the institutional development of the modern bourgeois hegemonic apparatus as a «practical and theoretical activity with which the ruling class not only justifies and maintains its dominance, but manages to win the active consent of those over whom it rules» (*ibid.*). In the Gramscian framework, however, the specificity of the biopolitical as an activity that maintains dominance would remain illegible and unaddressed. From the Foucaultian perspective of the socialization and universalization of the bourgeois mode of production, the biopolitical is the pinnacle of modern capitalist efficiency, reproduction, and domination. Gramsci is largely praised for the originality of his critique of Marxist "economism" prior to the 1930s. In contrast to Nicos Poulantzas in *Political Power and Social Classes* (1973), who argued that the concept of hegemony should only apply to the practices of the dominant classes, Foucault invites us to revisit the very relation between calculation, politics and the production of bodies, institutions and specific valorizations of the idea of "life".

However, in his 2009 book *The Gramscian Moment: Philosophy, Hegemony and Marxism* Peter Thomas recognizes in passing the significance of "biopolitics" for the study of the modern and contemporary parameters of hegemony though he chooses to do so without mentioning Foucault by name. Instead, Thomas references the phenomenon, establishes its relation to Gramsci's prior formulation of the "hegemonic apparatus" in *The Prison Notebooks*, and immediately rejects any potential Foucaultian legacy for the present or future consideration of hegemony, and, presumably, for the development of any form of Gramsci-inflected Marxism in general. Thomas frames his brief approach to biopolitics in the following terms:

> Gramsci's concept of a hegemonic apparatus can be comprehended as a realistic translation of the themes that have more recently been proposed under the thesis of *biopower* and *biopolitics*; a thesis that remains, in my view, despite its proponents' claims, overdetermined by the modern conception of sovereignty that obscures the specific nature of *class* power" (2009, p. 225).

As far as Thomas is concerned, Gramsci's concept of the "hegemonic apparatus" is a superior formulation since it is "realistic", whereas, presumably, biopolitics is either not realistic or somehow less realistic than Gramsci's formulations regarding the passive revolution, civil society, and the integral state in *The Prison Notebooks*. Perhaps Thomas means that Gramsci's "hegemonic apparatus" actually "names" and therefore represents and subsumes "material reality" in ways that "biopolitics" does not. But this question, which is ultimately a question concerning the terms of submission to, or refusal of, a master language, be it that of empiricity in general or that of the particular surname "Gramsci", remains unaddressed.

Thomas' passing comment is not without its blind spots. For example his claim to realism, that is, his dismissal of biopolitics as a possible pathway toward the further critical consideration not only of the "hegemonic apparatus", but of hegemony itself, is, despite his claims, clearly overdetermined by: (1) a logically impossible inversion in the relations of translation between Gramsci and Foucault, in the sense that history teaches us that it is the latter that translates the former, not the other way around; (2) an overriding desire to guarantee the paternity of the Gramscian signature over all others, in the process suturing contemporary

Marxism's philological fidelity in absolutely orthodox ways to a single master language (given the consciously provisional nature of Gramsci's writings and principle formulations throughout *The Prison Notebooks*, this seems to be a particularly problematic gesture); (3) an apparent unawareness of the details of Foucault's arguments regarding the nature of "class" power in the lectures presented by Foucault in *Society Must Be Defended* and *The Birth of Biopolitics*.

However, in his precipitous dismissal of both Michel Foucault and the questions raised by the phenomenon of biopolitics, Peter Thomas has touched upon a productive tension underlying the relation between the Gramscian understanding of the "hegemonic apparatus" and Foucault's formulation of the biopolitical. Thomas clearly seeks to cast biopolitics into oblivion in the name of the superiority of the plausible, that is, "real politics", though it remains unclear what he understands by this.

There is, however, something fundamental (rather than merely displaceable) in the relation between Gramsci's "hegemonic apparatus" and Foucault's approach to biopolitics. For Gramsci, of course, the 'hegemonic apparatus' referred to the mediations of social class at the heart of the modern integral state via the forging across civil society of the educational apparatus (school, university), the cultural apparatus (museums, libraries etc.), the organization of information, the everyday environment, town planning, and the traditional apparatuses of the Church and the intellectuals (Buci-Glucksmann, 1980, p. 48). In his lectures on biopolitics it is patently clear that Foucault is striving to supplement rather than to ignore, displace or invalidate Gramsci's formulations regarding the "hegemonic apparatus", the "passive revolution", or the "revolution without revolution". It is equally clear that in his lectures the class power of the bourgeoisie is absolutely central to the emergence, extension and naturalization of the biopolitical realm from the eighteenth to the twentieth century. As already suggested, biopolitics in Foucault is the name of the process by which the bourgeoisie utilizes the truth of calculation (*ratio*, technology) in order to orient the human – the human as subject and object of production simultaneously – toward specific "ways of life" that are internal to the unfolding of the modern integral state in the epoch of the technological development of the bourgeois mode of production, of the fetishization of the commodity-form, and of the accomplished and fully socialized reification of the human body in its relation to the full technical realization of surplus value.

Through biopolitics, calculation and logistical certainty are applied and implemented for the benefit of bourgeois command, for the constant surmounting by the subject of all forms of social "arbitrariness", and for the fully regularized and naturalized advancement of social stability, population management and anthropological reproduction. Biopolitics is a supplementary term, in other words, for Gramsci's approach to the emergent hegemony of the "passive revolution" and the "integral state". As such, it is also a synonym for the reduction of human existence to the will to power of modern bourgeois forms of subjectivity and modern capitalist technicity. For this reason it could be said that biopolitics names the forms of demographic calculation by means of which the technological advances that inspired the autonomy of the machinic – an emergent autonomy that was central to the expansion of the factory regime during industrial modernity – also penetrated the body and mind not just of the worker in the factory but of the entire population "beyond" the confines of the factory walls.

In contrast to Thomas' formulation, then, biopolitics is integral to the unveiling, rather than to the obfuscation, of the specific nature of class power understood as a modern ethical force not only in the institutions of civil society and the political state, but also in the economic production of bodies and consciousness. In Gramsci, the hegemonic apparatus forges the institutions of civil society. In Foucault, biopolitics supplements Gramsci's perspective on the formation of the integral state (in which political society + civil society = the integral state) by focusing on the economization of "life itself". Foucault was aware, in other words, that whereas the mere preservation of power is akin to a decrease in power, biopolitics is predicated on the constant "enhancement" of power via the bourgeois socialization of anticipatory security, counting, calculating, predicting, pre-empting, constantly reorienting the subject to what is certain, foreseeable, and correct according to the truth of *ratio*. It is in this sense that the biopolitical *ratio* extends itself throughout the social sphere "against" divergence, arbitrariness, or, for that matter, any possible coming of an event, for while the event is the co-emergence of the act of naming and of the thing named, biopolitics is designed to veil access to both the arbitrariness of the signifier and indeed to the signified, in order to emphasize pre-emptively the regularization of preconceived notions of subjectivity, order and "ways of life" grounded in certainty, regulation and reproductive value. Biopolitical hegemony is not about the imposition or coercion of a dominant ideology (Marx) or the extension of specific mechanisms of political legitimacy (Weber). It is about the everyday normalization and peaceful regularization of ideology, coercion, domination and legitimacy. And it can do this because it mobilizes the relation between life and death (existence) in a previously unseen manner, by placing it at the heart of modern production itself.

Ontologically, biopolitics functions only ever on the side of the ontic, though Foucault himself never addressed specifically the question of biopolitics as ontological closure. He never considered the fact that the biopolitical veils the question of existence and subsumes it under the administration of technique and calculative reason. He preferred to stay away from the very question in life for the essence of death in order to remain within the historicist field of the sociological. For this reason, in Foucault property and value take absolute precedence over the ontological presuppositions of each and every possible existential analytic, and in his lectures any potential decision for the question of existence remains foreclosed by the positive production of the bourgeois subject and its ways of life, as both historical reality and as the sociological object of analysis.

Foucault's approach to the biopolitical is, to an extent at least, Gramscian (that is, sociological). But it is also potentially post-Gramscian since it carries within itself the opportunity to take the fabrication of hegemony beyond the political society/civil society relation (beyond, that is, the purely sociological realm) and into the realm of the technological subsumption of existence via the forging of new sovereign ways of making live and of letting die. By this I mean to indicate that while Foucault's examination of biopolitics makes mortality itself the sociological drama of the political sphere, it simultaneously orients the thinking of that same political sphere away from the ontological presuppositions that allows us to posit the question of mortality in the first place. Foucault's analysis is itself an exercise in biopolitical production and oblivion (historicism, sociology, anthropology, humanism) in which the social physics of the biopolitical strives, but ultimately fails, to contain the constitutive question of metaphysics.

Biopolitics therefore not only remains consciusly blind to the ontological problematic; it is that blindness reconverted into the socialization of the everyday and the sociologization of political thinking itself. It therefore posits, on one side, the technologically mediated subordination of the workers' body reconverted into the calculability of the value of life on a previously unseen and unimaginable scale, and, on the other, the relation between the political and its ontological presuppositions to the extent that it is itself the subtraction of the relation between life and death from every ontological presupposition in favor of the absolute economization and circulation of mortality in the name of the extension and reproduction of surplus value. For this reason I would propose that all contemporary thinking of the limits of the political would do well to consider the possibility of a post-Gramscian and of a post-Foucaultian inflection, in such a way as to think both the limits "of" and "between" hegemony and biopolitics. I will return to this inflection shortly.

In contrast to what Peter Thomas thinks, biopolitics for Foucault is clearly the positing of a specific moment in the history of private property, of the economization of technology and of the systemic reduction of existence to the omnipotence of production, exchange value and use value. As such, it is internal to and constitutive of the modern development of the technologies of capitalist power and domination as well as to the concomitant expropriation of existence in the name of private property, understanding that expropriation as the social saturation of specifically bourgeois (that is, of fully individualized and privatized) ways of life. It signals, therefore, the advent of a new epoch of bondage not only to wage labor but to fertility, birth, safety, security, insurance, healthcare, sexual normativity, medicalization, police regulation, the enhancement, extension and penetrative force of technicity, and the reification of the human body in general.

At the time of Foucault's lectures in the 1970s Marxism scarcely had a vocabulary capable of addressing such questions with any degree of specificity. It understood that private property was the forced self-estrangement of man, certainly, and that Communism signified the ideal negation of the negation of the subject, the historical passage from alienation to humanity (a fully objective and therefore represented species-man), but it could do little to counter the emerging realization that alongside capitalism the history of Actually Existing Socialism had also developed internally to the historical universalization of biopolitical technicity. The question of human alienation had not been resolved, in other words, from within the social and political histories opened up by the 1917 October Revolution. In *Capital* Marx had acknowledged the debt of communism to capitalism, without doubt, and, indeed, in "The Economic and Philosophical Manuscripts" had touched upon what can now be recognized as one of the foundational problems for the transcendental promise of communism (even though for decades it was taken to be the gospel truth), when he observed that: «The supersession (*Aufhebung*) of self-estrangement takes the same course as self-estrangement» (1844, p. 345). For Heidegger this amounted to admitting that no revolution could ever really be revolutionary enough, which is precisely where he would position himself in relation to the Marxian legacy in "The Letter on Humanism" (1998) and elsewhere.

With this unresolved yet fundamental question regarding the supersession of self-estrangement from within the history of self-estrangement itself in mind (in which the entirety of human history is placed essentially at the feet of the Hegelian dialectic, and, as such, at the feet of the understanding of the entirety of human history as a history of causality and Spirit) Kostas Axelos observed just a few years before Foucault first formulated his lectures on biopolitics, that Marx did not «see to the very end the way in which socialism, communism and practical materialism are the *heirs* of the bourgeoisie, capitalism, and positivism» (1976, p. 306). Marx was not, continued Axelos in what was an utterly dumbfounding proposition for the time, «someone to whom it was given to understand that the so-called bourgeois forms of life are more fit to survive than the bourgeoisie itself. And so he refused to see in the new society a fundamental democratization and universalization of 'bourgeois forms', a continuation of this strange, solid, errant 'bourgeoisie' – with or without bourgeois man himself» (*ibid.*). In other words, it was not given to Marx to think the full extension of alienation, preferring instead to promise the coming ontic supersession of that alienated subject in the name of a fully transcendental species-man, future total man, or Spirit. Marx's entanglements with alienation, for Axelos, ended up veiling the existential question of alienation since «Marx's answers to critical questions too often lie on a level different from that of the question itself" (p. 320).

In the orthodoxies of the 1970s state hegemony was understood in Gramscian terms, and it was commonly held that Marx's humanism – his quest for a fully unalienated humanity, or metaphysics – would emancipate both subjectivity and technology from all particular or private appropriations. But there was no detailed accounting from within Marxism itself of either the biopolitical supersession of the biopolitical or of the day-to-day *ratio* of what Axelos formulated as that strange, solid "errant bourgeoisie" functioning on behalf of the full socialization of the means of production, with or without bourgeois man himself. I would posit that Axelos' strange solid "errant bourgeoisie" – the persistence beyond the presence of bourgeois man himself of what he referred to as "bourgeois forms of life" – is precisely what Foucault would refer to just a few years later as biopolitical regularization. I would also posit that Gramscian Marxism has not accounted for this question in any detail, and, indeed, that contemporary philological Marxism remains ill equipped to do so.

Despite all claims to Gramscian realism, it is through biopolitics that we can glimpse the fact that the socialization of the means of production might not lead inevitably to the end of alienation and exploitation, since it would still develop internally to the realm of *techne*. We also see that it is not enough to reduce our understanding of hegemony to the institutions of the integral pedagogical state. It is therefore thanks in part to Foucault (while also recognizing the need to move beyond Foucault) that we can now lend an ear to an added level of complexity in what Gramsci called the passive revolution of the integral nation state, understanding it not only as an institutional shift in the sovereign will to power but also as a shift in the human-technicity relation itself, a process in which Marx's quest for the fully un-estranged subject remains to this day overdetermined by the systemic rationalization of naturalized and normalized bourgeois subjective forms and "ways of life" in both the capitalist and formerly socialist worlds. In both worlds (though certainly with different governmental techniques) the great regulative idea of biopolitics would, it was thought, reconcile body, mind, and consciousness to each other in the name of the full extension of specific subject formations and ways of life, while all reifications of the human would reconcile human existence with (private or state-run) production alone. However, the political reconciliation of subjectivity, production and world only ever presupposes a masterful arrangement and modulation of force. It presupposes the existence of directive ideas, and therefore of hegemony.

Marx advocated the historical transcendence of the capital-labor relation as the directive idea of Communism. His nihilism was predicated on the optimism of pessimism and the idea of a destructive path to transcendence, which he understood as the dictatorship of the proletariat capable of suppressing each and every attempt to reinstate private property. Biopolitics, in contrast, works on the side of general ontic equivalence and the closure of all transcendence via the privatization of experience. It sides, in other words, with the ontic regularization of alienation, with the veiling of destruction and its reconversion into preordained understandings of "productive life". In this process of veiling, capitalism produces itself as the only plausible reality available, normalizing the absolute nearness and intimacy of commodity fetishism in everyday life, consciousness, and language while working in full conjunction with an ever increasing distancing of thinking from the possibility of emancipation from the conditions of that everydayness. Biopolitics, in this sense, is a name for the historical, social, economic and cultural realignment of the mind and body to the exigencies of the normalization of commodity fetishism, of instinct subsumed to production, and of existence conquered by technique and calculation. Of course communism and socialism were never a stranger to the biopolitical extension of Axelos' strange solid "errant bourgeoisie", despite all claims to the contrary.

But all of this is lost entirely on the philological fidelity that overdetermines Peter Thomas' precipitous displacement of the biopolitical in the name of the law of the Gramscian signature and the sociological plausibility of the "hegemonic apparatus"; an insistence on a "real politics" that is designed to metaphorize and thereby render fully legible the sociological, historicist and institutional path along which the self-estranged subaltern classes must learn to travel in order to cease to be subaltern, overcome their conditions of subjective self-estrangement, and thereby become dominant. In this sense the supersession of subalternity takes exactly the same temporal-historical course as domination, and the political is placed in its entirety – as "realism" and "actuality" – once again at the feet of the Hegelian dialectical life of Spirit. Revolutionary politics is the expropriation of the expropriators in the name of the supersession of subjective alienation and the coming into being of humanity as an absolutely collectivized and generalized objective, that is, represented, general equivalence. In this process bourgeois biopolitical regularization – the strange, solid, errant "bourgeoisie" given over to the production of technique and of technological subjectification – anchors its survival in a new form, as subaltern domination, or hegemony, in the logical subalternization of the former expropriators. For this reason the revolutionary politics of the acquisition of state power is the active containment – the enclosing within the enclosure itself – of the relation between subject and object, or dominance and subordination, within the same hermeneutic circle of *techne*. Everything inside that circle is the modern work of regularization (the violence of legislative normativity, the hegemony of the biopolitical itself in both capitalist and socialist conditions) or naked force.

Marcus Green observes that what Gramsci had in mind in his approach to the passive revolution and the integral state was the formation of an "ethical State", and he describes Gramsci's ethical state as «a state that can transform the oppressive state and transform the relations of subordination that created and perpetuated group marginalization» (p. 22). Green then goes on to cite Gramsci's own formulation of the "ethical State" in the following terms: «[T]he social group that poses the end of the State and its own end as the target to be achieved can create an ethical State – i.e. one which tends to put an end to the internal divisions of the ruled, etc., and to create a technically and morally unitary social organism» (Gramsci, 1971, p. 259, Notebook 9, §179); (*ibid.*). Green then closes with the following formulation regarding Gramsci's notion of the ethical state: «What Gramsci has in mind is a postsubaltern state, a democratic state that disallows the domination of one group by another» (*ibid.*).

With this formulation in mind, we can presume that Gramsci's ethical "postsubaltern" state would be a "democratized" state. However, from within the hermeneutic circle, or *techne*, of the subject-object, domination-subordination, hegemony-subalternity relation, it would not necessarily be a "democratizing" state actively seeking to disallow domination. Since by definition "hegemony" can change the conditions of, but cannot disallow, domination – because it is itself the organization of the techniques of repression, or common sense, at any given time – the integrative power of Gramsci's ethical state could be just as prone to representational ossification, normativity, conformism and totalization as any "oppressive state". For this reason, perhaps it could be suggested that what Gramsci might have had in mind ultimately for the "ethical State", but that remained unarticulated in his writings, was not hegemony but "posthegemony", that is, the conceptual terrain of a ceaseless deconstruction of the conditions of mediated subordination and of the technical domination of one group by another, in such a way as to conceive of democracy as unceasing "democratization".

Posthegemony is the ceaseless de-metaphorization of the legislative and representational order (or *nomos*) that structures hegemony – the gathering of logos, of the filial, friendship, the subjectum of representation – and the normalizing biopolitical anthropologism that underlies and naturalizes it. In this context, perhaps only "posthegemony" would have the ability to deliver on the ultimate horizon of Gramsci's ethical State since it de-metaphorizes and unworks hegemony and hegemony thinking, both of which are predicated, as already suggested, on the regularization of the bourgeois subject even in its most politically militant forms. By definition, in other words, the will to power that underlies every hegemony can only ever thwart the structural promise of what Marcus Green refers to as Gramsci's postsubaltern state.

What, then, can we understand by "posthegemony"? Posthegemony is, in the horizon of the *status quo* of contemporary planetary *techne*, the promise of a democratization of democracy through the de-metaphorization of the metaphysics of gathering (*koinon*). For this reason more than the question of the State the phenomenon of "populism" and its relation to, and potential distance from, the perpetuation of the modern hegemony of anthropological subjectivism – for example, of the fortification of political discourse around the cult of personality and the calculated language of "us versus them", or of "friend versus enemy", which exists on both "Right" "and" "Left" – is central to the concerns of posthegemonic thinking. Posthegemony considers the communal proximity inherent in our understanding of the word "We" – when taken and extended, that is, in the historical and conceptual framework and metaphysical habitus of the *pros hen* (the One) – to be the most dangerous of words. For that reason posthegemony is the thinking not of belonging or of the "supersession of self-estrangement", but of what Kostas Axelos referred to (following one strand within Heidegger's existential analytic) as the «uncanny homeland of homeless modern humans» (2015, p. 116).

While both hegemony and biopolitics represent the politics of gathering, communion, commonality, certainty, and actualization – that is, of presence – and while in both hegemony and biopolitics the question of existence remains subsumed by a globalization arranged through the technological life-forms of its errant bourgeoisie, posthegemony strives to traverse the enclosure of *techne* «up to its very boundaries and to trace the internal disturbances of its arrangements» (Schürmann, 2003, p. 522). For this reason alone, in the era of planetary *techne* the exploration of the infrapolitical resources and violent marks of posthegemony – that is, of the uncanny aporias of existential homelessness – is crucial. After all, everything else is just contemporary regularization (subsumption), naked force, and the sociological impasses of "realistic" – subjectivist, plausible – politics.

References

Axelos K. (1976). *Alienation, Praxis, and Techne in the Thought of Karl Marx*. Austin: University of Texas Press.
Buci-Glucksmann C. (1980). *Gramsci and the State*. London: Lawrence and Wishart.
Foucault M. (2003). *"Society Must Be Defended": Lectures at the Collège de France, 1975-76*. New York: Picador.
Foucault M. (2008). *The Birth of Biopolitics: Lectures at the Collège de France, 1978-1979*. New York: Palgrave Macmillan.
Gramsci A. (1971). *Selections from the Prison Notebooks*. New York: International Publishers.
Gramsci A. (2007). *Prison Notebooks*. Vols. 1-3. New York: Columbia University Press.
Green M. (2002). Gramsci Cannot Speak: Presentations and Interpretations of Gramsci's Concept of the Subaltern. *Rethinking Marxism*, 14/3: 1-14.
Heidegger M. (1998). The Letter on Humanism. In: *Pathmarks*, ed. by W. McNeill. Cambridge: Cambridge University Press: 239-276.
Marx K. (1992). Economic and Philosophical Manuscripts (1844). In: *Early Writings*. London: Penguin Books: 279-400.
Marx K. (1993). *Foundations of the Critique of Political Economy*. London: Penguin Books.
Poulantzas N. (1978). *Political Power and Social Classes*. New York: Verso.
Schürmann R. (2003). *Broken Hegemonies*. Bloomington, IN: Indiana University Press.
Thomas P.D. (2010). *The Gramscian Moment: Philosophy, Hegemony and Marxism*. Chicago: Haymarket Books.

Alberto Moreiras
HEGEMONY AND KATAPLEXIS

Perry Anderson's recent *The H-Word. The Peripeteia of Hegemony* (2017) may serve, perhaps paradoxically, to introduce a short and clear definition of posthegemony that might perhaps be common to the different positions a further elaboration could establish and convey. My interest in this paper is simply to bring out something like the basic conditions of the notion, its minimal features, so that we can move past the various misunderstandings that have plagued discussion so far.

Anderson's fundamental interest is geopolitical. He pays a larger attention, not to the Gramscian version of hegemony theory, or to Ernesto Laclau's, but to the history of uses of the term "hegemony" in the academic field of international relations, from the 1930s on, but especially after World War II. It comes as no surprise that North American analysts are dominant in Anderson's analysis. His interest, as a consequence, studies the international relations history of North American power from the perspective of its self-perception, essentially from the War to the present. I will bypass most of those analyses for the sake of a narrower focus.

In its Greek origins "hegemony" struggled to differentiate itself semantically from a word that was most clearly connected with rule, that is, *arkhé*. Anderson shows that, insofar as it concerns North American hegemonic power, even in our days there is a fundamental ambiguity as to the difference, or the proximity, between hegemony and empire. It is therefore pertinent that Anderson refers to a famous fragment from Diodorus Siculus. The fragment says: «Those who wish to achieve hegemony acquire it with valor and intelligence (*andreia kai sunesis*), increase it with moderation and benevolence (*epieikeia kai philanthropoia*), and maintain it with fear and paralysing terror (*phobos kai kataplexis*)» (2017, p. 182). *Kataplexis*, rendered by Anderson as "paralysing terror", is, Anderson remarks, the "last word" of hegemony, certainly the "last word" of the "war on terror", «war as terror, without boundary or end» (p. 183). The notion of posthegemony is radically connected to an understanding of hegemony as structurally sustained on terror, hence a desire to do without hegemony for the sake of democratic politics.

Some will argue that the strong association of hegemony and terror is counterintuitive and somewhat arbitrary. After all, many of those today known as fervid supporters of the notion of hegemony in the Marxist or post-Marxist tradition would deny it or would do whatever possible to avoid it. Hegemony, for them, is the very opposite of terror, it is rather rule by persuasion and consent, voluntary servitude or voluntary subjection, and, insofar as it be voluntary, never subjected to the anxiety of terror. Hegemony is, today, perhaps, in its counterhegemonic version (that is, not hegemony as already accomplished, rather hegemony as what is to be accomplished, against some previous, and agonizing or dead, hegemony), the key word of what is understood by Left – at least it is the key word in the Latin American left, no less than in the Spanish left represented by Podemos. The question to them is what would they do if forced to recognize that the notion of hegemony cannot be cleansed of its contamination by a form of rule that, in interstate relations, has a non-deniable link with despotic authority. Paralysing terror, in Anderson's story, is only the final truth of an endemic conflict – the conflict of politics – that hegemony disavows by potentially, tendentially, or actually crushing its antagonists: *kataplexis* indeed. Hegemony unconceals itself as *kataplexis*. In every case.

We started using the term "posthegemony" as a result of readings and conversations and discussions held towards the end of the 1990s, already twenty years ago, in the context of our interest in the work to be done by the Latin American Subaltern Studies Group. The Latin Americanist group started off as an attempt to imitate (I suppose, *mutatis mutandis*) the project carried out by the South Asian Subaltern Studies Group, a mostly Indian collective that had been founded by the Bengali historian Ranajit Guha at the University of Sussex at the end of the 1970s. His important book,

Dominance without Hegemony (1997), must be mentioned here as a book that anchored many of the discussions; just as many, perhaps, as Gayatri Chakravorty Spivak's 1985 article "Subaltern Studies: Deconstructing Historiography" (1988). Guha's collective was openly inspired by Antonio Gramsci's Marxism, but the South Asian group was largely dissident from the Marxist orthodoxy of the time. Spivak, just as an example, was primarily interested in deconstruction, although with a clear political commitment both through Marxism and feminism. In Anderson's words, «under the impact of post-structuralism, there was an increasing turn to discursive constructions of power and cultural rather than material determinants of consciousness or action» (Anderson, 2017, p. 100). Granted that intellectual developments always take a little time to find their way into the more or less lethargic Latin Americanist academy, what was clear for the South Asians «at the end of the eighties» (*ibid.*) was still hazy for the Latin Americanist subalternists in the mid-1990s. A conflict, within the latter group, between traditional Marxism and the "post-structuralism" Anderson invokes was inevitable. But this could still be a rather reductive way of putting it.

To say that poststructuralism was dominant in the academic milieu of the 1990s is of course a blatant exaggeration. It simply had a certain prestige among an intellectual elite that, in our field, has nothing to do with the conventional professorial ranks: indeed, for work in Latin American or Hispanic studies, the "best" universities have frequently been among the most backward and reactionary, as it is still very much the case today. When the field shows an interest in "subaltern studies" in the mid 1990's, it does so, to a certain extent, out of a certain knee-jerk desire to borrow some of the prestige attached to the revisionist (post-)Marxism of the South Asian group. Yes, there were a few things in orthodox Marxism that were crumbling everywhere and of which nobody wanted to make themselves responsible. Eurocommunism, even, had been biting the dust in elections in Southern Europe for about 15 years, and most communist parties in the West were undergoing effective collapse – something that was not solely caused by the fall of the Berlin Wall and the dissolution of the Soviet empire. At the time there were in fact only a few variants of Marxism that retained public *caché*: *operaismo* in general, that is, postdialectical Marxisms represented by thinkers such as Mario Tronti, Antonio Negri, Massimo Cacciari, and Fredric Jameson's openly culturalist and antipolitical Marxism. Marxism was not quite dead, but it was not precisely thriving. Although of course there were many intellectuals who wanted to salvage their own Marxist and political commitments. It would be a few years before the *sui-generis* Marxisms or post-Marxisms of people like Slavoj Žižek, Alain Badiou, or Jacques Rancière, among others, recovered an impact for Marxism that had briefly seemed lost – but this partial or diagonal resuscitation of Althusserianism was not particularly relevant for South Asian subalternism, more attuned to the Birmingham School tradition and the work of Raymond Williams and Stuart Hall. Postcolonial cultural studies were taking off, and figures like Homi Bhabha were acquiring influence.

South Asian subalternists were not alien to these events or this state of affairs – many of them taught in the West. To use Williams' categories, many were caught between a residual Marxism and an emergent post-Marxism that, in some but not all cases, evolved unhappily towards a culturalism that was strongly inspired by North American-style "identity politics". In fact, most postcolonial thought of the period can only be analysed as a variation on the identity-politics basic score. Deconstruction was there through Spivak, as already mentioned, and Dipesh Chakrabarty was interested in Heideggerian phenomenology. Gyan Prakash was more of a culturalist, whereas Partha Chatterjee was closer to straightforward Marxist historiography. When all these theoretical ambiguities and options reach the time of their purported adoption by Latin American Studies – that is, by a small and in fact rather marginal group in the field –, they would only become accentuated as ambiguities. In the Latin Americanist case, beyond a residual Marxism that had been taking it severely on the neck given a number of political disasters in Central America, and the negative impact of the Cuban "special period", there was a strong underlying and endemic identitarianism that predated even North American varieties. And the antitheoretical bias in the field is well known. Generally speaking, the Latin Americanist *rapprochement* to South Asian subalternism was perhaps even unconsciously identitarian, so radically culturalist, and certainly not very explicitly interested in what Anderson calls "material determinants of consciousness or action" except in a banal or generic sense. It was anybody's guess as to what would happen when, at a second moment of constitution, a number of younger scholars entered the group with an intellectual agenda that was not Marxist to start with (although they were not anti-Marxist); that had in fact formulated critiques, and that came to subalternism through those critiques, concerning Marxist productionism and Marxist anthropological subjectivism and Marxist philosophy of history; that had no particular interest, in fact, that came to subalternism given their lack of interest in culturalism of any kind; and whose relationship to any and all identitarianisms, particularly when camouflaged as political commitment or political action, was clearly skeptical or even antagonistic. Tensions would flare up soon.

At the time of the unavoidable intergenerational confrontation in 1998 the Latin American Subaltern Studies Group would break into three fragments: one of them, substantially the founding group, characterized by a culturalist Marxism, or rather a Marxist culturalism; the second one, postcolonial identitarian; and the third one would take some time to find its name, and finds it eventually in the midst of some disagreement: posthegemonic subalternism, which understood first of all that no culturalism could ever satisfy it. Of course the larger group cannot survive the explosion, and it can and should be said that after 1998 there is no properly so-called Latin Americanist subalternism. The non-culturalist splinter group could only use the tag "posthegemony" at times, since not everybody was in agreement on it. But, in terms of those who were, two different forms of understanding the term emerged: one, under the influence of Antonio Negri's *operaismo* and Pierre Bourdieu's sociology, would result in Jon Beasley-Murray's understanding and in his 2010 book *Posthegemony: Political Theory and Latin America*. The second tendency would have to do more with Derridean deconstruction – obviously no belief in hegemonic power in it – and it is the tendency I favor, although I hope that any posthegemonic tendency (there are several; see Castro, 2015) will accept the comments that follow. It should not be necessary to repeat that posthegemony, in either of those two versions, was no longer subalternist, since it constituted itself in a process of explicit rupture with a subalternism that did not include only the elder Latin Americanist culturalists but that also underwent a process of critique vis-à-vis the South Asian work, including Guha's, but also Chakrabarty, Prakash, and Chatterjee's among others. Ours was a different project, from a different social and political history, a different intellectual genealogy, and different existential and philosophical projections. The point of radical agreement could be said to be the rejection of voluntary servitude in any way or manner: posthegemony is first of all, and perhaps also last of all, a refusal to submit (not a heroic refusal; just a factic refusal, out of tiredness and boredom) to any unexamined social or political or institutional power.

The understanding of hegemony as an *ideologem* intrinsically connected to the history of domination meant that there was a link between hegemony and the history of metaphysics. Martin Heidegger's cryptic but nevertheless incisive destruction of hegemony in connection with the history of the false in the West in his 1942 book *Parmenides* (1998) was perhaps determinant for this. The attempt to elaborate not a political theory rather simply a political position that could be consistent and commensurate with the thematics of ontological destruction in post-Heideggerian thought, including deconstruction, suggested that hegemony was not a conceptual tool that should remain immune to criticism. We were assiduous readers of Ernesto Laclau and Chantal Mouffe's work, but had never been convinced that political articulation could be finally identified in any way or manner with hegemony theory. We learned a lot from Laclau and Mouffe about a certain factical stance in politics such as it happens, and we read Laclau against himself by positing the possibility that subalternity should be considered a non-recuperable, non-hegemonizable constitutive outside of any hegemony and of any hegemonic pretense – something for which the already mentioned essay by Gayatri Spivak gave us the clue. Guha's book, on "dominance without hegemony" (1997) also gave us important insights in spite of a number of things we had to disagree with. We could all be more or less in agreement that hegemony theory, in its Guhan or Laclauian versions, was useful to understand historical processes concerning power formations but, if hegemony theory was going to end up proposing, for instance, that any political solution would go through the construction of articulatory chains of counterhegemonic demands under a leader in the usurpatory function of empty signifier, that was not a solution we could ever feel enthusiastic about. It seemed to condemn us politically to what was already intolerable at the analytic level, which was the absolute privilege of the identitarian demand. And it seemed to condemn us to what seemed politically intolerable, namely, the infinite process of waiting for the leader, for the *parousia* of an always seedy charisma that had to be guaranteed, or invented, or in any case forcibly sustained (no defeatism, please!) as an unconditional demand of the theory itself. Not for us.

I should add that, at least in my case, the notion of posthegemony had no pretensions in terms of becoming a political theory or a theory of the political. It was not a matter of opposing a posthegemony theory to the already formalized Laclauian theory of hegemony. Posthegemony was, and continues to be, an analytic vector whose destructive function should be addressed to any power pretensions – political, social, institutional, intellectual. It was a tool for deconstruction, a notion that enabled a particular stance within the political text, or within the politico-cultural text, if you want, an extension beyond the literary to what had already been rehearsed many times on the literary or the critical text. Posthegemony was minimally a critical resource against any legitimation of power and domination. If hegemony, in any discursive formation, referred, always and in every case, to an implicit or explicit hegemonic principle, and if around such hegemonic principle an ideology could consolidate whose function necessarily was the retention of power in the immediate subalternization of any ideological outside, then posthegemony was, minimally, but not unimportantly, and not tamely, a resistance to subalternization and a resistance to the mandate for voluntary servitude: a sort of an-archy, not in the traditional anarchist sense, rather in the sense of the refusal of any *arkhé* as *arkhé*. It inverted the sign of equivalential construction from what Laclau liked to call its "constitutive outside": in posthegemony, the equivalential construction is always on the side of the subaltern. Spivak had argued in her already mentioned 1985 essay that the subaltern position was structurally a position that could not be narrativized by any logic of power, that is, a position always excluded from power narratives – this was of course a strong, even decisive correction to the conventional notion that the subaltern is the necessary correlative of hegemony, that the subaltern is precisely the field of action of hegemony as such. Posthegemony, then, wonders whether it is possible to extract political energy from exclusion as such, from a state of denarrativization or prenarrativization, from a radical tropological outside; that is, from a savage and nameless hybridity, as I had attempted to say in the last chapter of my 2001 book *The Exhaustion of Difference*, always previous to any construction of a political subject. Posthegemony attempts to endow subaltern political vectors with dignity, to the very extent that they have not yet entered processes of subjective articulation, which are always hegemonizing processes.

I will not hesitate to call Perry Anderson' *The H-Word* (2017) a decisively posthegemonic book, given the fact that it is structured around the dangerous ambiguity between hegemony and empire, which Anderson shows is sustained alongside the history of the concept in diverse ways, even if some times in a (falsely) denegated or repressed way. But the corollary of the ambiguity between hegemony and empire, or between hegemony and power, is: *kataplexis*. It should not surprise that hegemony may have been all along a thought of domination – rather, what is surprising is the leftist cant that allows one to think that you can have hegemony without domination. The instance of domination in hegemonic power cannot be denied, much less denegated – only theoreticians already compromised by their nearness to political power, such as Joseph Nye, can propose the notion that hegemony is "soft power", power without power, the pure generous friendship of the hegemon. Certainly hegemony proponents, whether at the intra- or inter-state levels, can feed their illusion that there are dominations and dominations, and that some are kinder and more amiable than others, and they are not entirely wrong of course. But that does not imply that hegemony theory will not return in every case to the heart of the old notion of politics as state action, as search for the exclusive monopoly of violence, which is never but the interest of the rich seeking domination over everyone else, to quote Machiavelli. But posthegemony is always on the side of those who do not want to be dominated. Posthegemony is resolutely on the side of the rejection of domination, and it is in that sense not just democratic thought, but a hyperbolic condition of democracy: there is no democracy without posthegemony, even though there may be posthegemony without democracy. Hegemons in Pericles' Greece were the ones considered possible bearers of the *arkhé*, that is, the principle of command. The struggle for hegemony was the struggle for *arkhic* access, which is ultimately the reason why in Lenin the word, which had been the object of a number of discussions in nineteenth century philology, can be strongly associated with the formation of a social class destined to take on political power. Education had the dual mission of preparing counterhegemonic agents for an effective taking of power and of generating consent among the proletariat. Anderson says about Lenin's idea of revolution that it was

> [I]n prospect […] a "democratic dictatorship of the proletariat and the peasantry", the oxymoron signifying a political regime in which dictatorship – rule by force – would be exercised over enemy classes, that is feudal landowners and bourgeois capitalists, while hegemony – rule by consent – would govern the relations of the working class with allied classes, above all the peasantry which made up the overwhelming majority of the population (2017, p. 16).

It is important to emphasize that hegemony, in its first Marxist uses, had to do with the capacity to influence for domination (capacity to induce voluntary servitude) – domination through persuasion for the "allied classes" and domination by force concerning the enemy classes. The very Antonio Gramsci, who expanded the concept and gave it a much more central and systematic reach for communist strategy, according to Anderson, «never relinquished his belief that for a deeper understanding of hegemony, coercion could not be divorced from consent, cultural ascendancy from repressive capacity» (p. 23). Hegemony works through voluntary servitude, but it does it always through its capacity to impose, if the will fails, pure and simple submission through any available resource or method.

In Anderson's text there is an openly displayed anxiety that hegemony follows, from those parameters, a "fatal law" that matches the diachronic process noted in Diodorus Siculus' fragment: once in power, hegemony degenerates more or less gradually into «an instrument of tyranny and servitude» (p. 33), becomes the bearer and the carrier of empire as naked power. This is precisely what was denied – denegated – in the 1970s struggles inside and against Eurocommunism in the Italian Communist Party concerning Gramsci's legacy: it was important at the time to dissolve the relationship between hegemony and dictatorship of the proletariat, to suppress the second in favor of the first, now understood as a process merely internal to the democratic structures of a parliamentarian state. Laclau and Mouffe's work is a direct descendant of that particular crisis of late communism and it capitalizes on the abandonment of the dark face of hegemony, «bringing post-structuralism boldly to bear on the Marxist tradition, in political sympathy with what had been Eurocommunism, but in theoretical outlook now declaratively post-Marxist» (p. 93), on the abandonment of every type of class essentialism and on the renunciation to the Gramscian notion of "war of movement" (p. 94). The way was open – through denegation, however – for the invocation of a notion of hegemony without the teeth of domination, a notion of hegemony committed to the deepening of the "radical democracy" that, in Laclau and Mouffe's theorization, would come not to substitute but rather to incorporate socialism as one of its dimensions. In his last systematic work, *On Populist Reason*, Laclau (2007) would radicalize his notion of radical democracy into populism, understood now as the very definition of politics. Anderson remarks that, if all politics is populist, and if hegemony theory defines every political form, then both hegemony and populism become supernumerary concepts, without any specificity. Say politics and you are already saying both hegemony and populism. At this very moment, when Anderson, who recognizes the extraordinary way in which Laclau and Mouffe's theorizations anticipated (and influenced) the modalities of contestation to the historical cycle of neoliberalism in Latin American from the end of the 1990s, speaks about Podemos and says of the Spanish party that it constitutes the outright adoption of the Laclauian theory by a political force with massive popular support: «In Spain, the leaders of Podemos – they too with a season in Latin America behind them – based its strategy expressly on their [Laclau and Mouffe's] prescriptions for a hegemonic populism» (Anderson, 2017, p. 95). But this means – Podemos, which has so loudly critiqued the so-called Transition of 1978, has actively incorporated the crypt of the Spanish Communist Party at the time: the active denegation of the kataplexic moment of hegemony. Which ought to induce some melancholy.

We offer posthegemony. I would like to conclude emphasizing the sleight-of-hand Anderson attributes, as a consequence of his book's *longue durée,* at the intra-state level for Gramsci and Laclau and Mouffe, and at the inter-state level for some of the geopolitics and international relations scholars he studies, to hegemony theory in its attempt to make the rabbit of coercive domination disappear from hegemony's hat. The problem is not of course Gramsci, or the Italian Communist Party fending off its own vanishing act, or Laclau and Mouffe. The problem is that, fifty years later, the global left is more than ever dependent on that toothless interpretation of Gramsci's work. Anderson says: «Gramsci would have been astonished» (2017, p. 98). And the problem is, furthermore, that there is no guarantee that what starts off as a cute sleight-of-hand magic trick does not end up in the tragic prestidigitation of political reality – politics is always the place for the return of the repressed in theory. Posthegemony installs itself right there, at that very place, in order to say, like a gadfly that has no intention of going away, and for whoever is interested, if not for the ox himself, that not only there is no exhaustion of political space induced by a hegemonic articulation – «something always escapes» to quote Beasley-Murray (2010) – a constitutive remainder is left out, an outside that is and will always be the place of non-identitarian, non-captured subalternity, the *marrano* place; but also that in that movement of domination through excluding submission hegemony theory reveals its antidemocratic virtuality. This is the symptom of an endemic and central problem – precisely because not just denied but denegated – in the contemporary Left.

Posthegemony could insist in its hyperbolic commitment to democracy understood as the defense of those who prefer not to be dominated – that is why it is also anti-hegemonic and antibiopolitical, to the extent that biopolitics is the administration of the life of those administrable. Posthegemony has no interest in becoming a political theory – it is rather only a place for freedom as non-administration, for freedom as the only instance of legitimation in a world deprived of legitimate principles of rule (because *nadie es más que nadie*): against *kataplexis*, modestly, but also against every identitarian or culturalist dissimulation of entropic *kataplexis* at the heart of hegemony.

References

Anderson P. (2017). *The H-Word. The Peripeteia of Hegemony*. London: Verso.
Beasley-Murray J. (2010). *Posthegemony: Political Theory and Latin America*. Minneapolis, MN: University of Minnesota Press.
Castro R., ed. (2015). *Poshegemonía: El final de un paradigma de la filosofía política en América Latina*. Madrid: Biblioteca Nueva.
Guha R. (1997). *Dominance without Hegemony*. Cambridge, MA: Harvard University Press.
Heidegger M. (1998). *Parmenides*. Bloomington, IN: Indiana University Press.
Laclau E. (2007). *On Populist Reason*. London: Verso.
Moreires A. (2001). *The Exhaustion of Difference*. Durham: Duke University Press.
Spivak G.C. (1985). Subaltern Studies: Deconstructing Historiography. In: Guha R. and Spivak G.C. *Selected Subaltern Studies*. New York: Oxford University Press: 3-34.

Emanuela Fornari
CRISIS OF HEGEMONY
Between Populism and Neoliberalism

1. In this paper I intend to start from the complicity between populism and neoliberalism in fragmenting the social bond as mirror images of "emptiness". We will go on to examine the difference between the concept of people and the concept of nation, but especially what Gramsci would have called an "organic crisis": that is, a loss of *trust*. Following on this is the silence of nihilistic theoretical-emotional radicalism that reads the social bond in its affinity with the dimension of passions and affections but not that of *desire*.

Let us take the classic example of Ernesto Laclau, for whom the "social" does not exist, limiting himself to the antithesis friend/enemy, associated with a use of Gramsci in a dissolving function of class society. This perspective, as we shall see, does not grasp the dissolution of the social bond from the dimension of material interests, and therefore of institutions: in particular that decomposition of the institutional logics that today produces a radical absence of rules hidden by the growth of legislation and law. But above all, it does not grasp the other side of the dissolution of the social, that is, the emergence of the necessity of the charismatic figure. As we shall see in the conclusion, a possible alternative to today's populism could be republicanism, that is, a flexible institutionalism, a legacy of Italian, Spanish, and partly Germanic culture. We will therefore propose, as a provisional conclusion, the idea of the Roman republic as an alternative to the proliferation of the market and the proliferation of law, taking the mirroring of the market and law as destabilizing factors. In other words, we will try to grasp in the "city" the embryo of an urban and metropolitan federalism.

But let's proceed with order. The classical reading of populism as a hangover from the nineteenth century ignores the phenomenon of the classes as proposed by Laclau's post-Marxism and does not capture the failure of the liberal model and the Marxist model as theoretical approaches to reading the present. In fact, the anthropological and philosophical basis of contemporary populism is nihilistic, post-modern and was born from the institutional and political crisis of meaning in recent decades. In summary, the contemporary populist position, described for example by the aforementioned Laclau, appears as anti-rationalist, anti-Kantian and anti-normative. Contemporary populism, in fact, is born from the ashes of the traditional people destroyed by neoliberalism, in the form of the emergence of contingent and transient "peoples" that do not have the homogeneity of the *founding people*. Populism, therefore, is not in itself the scorned anti-politics, since the real anti-political force is the neoliberal market. If the matrix of anti-politics is neoliberalism, populism is the consequence. From this point of view populism (especially that theorized by Laclau) is an attempt to relaunch the "political" and to launch a new order on the basis of a post-metaphysical and post-fundamental order that insists on the *discursive* character of the people. As is well known, in fact, for Laclau the people are a failed "totality" built by political discourse.

2. If, as commonly argued, the media discourse is the main ground for the construction of populism, not enough attention has been given to the isomorphism between neoliberalism and populism: that is to say their genetic link. Returning to Laclau one can consider the central category of "demand" for him. If for Laclau the concept of "demand" indicates the claims of the "people", it is clear that the same concept has been central to the constitution of the "market" since its inception. It is from this point of view that we can speak of a structural and genetic link between populism and neoliberalism, that is, of an essential relationship between populism, capitalism and neoliberalism. From this point of view, populism can be read as the *form of politics* in the neoliberal era. The anthropological basis of neoliberalism on which populism is grafted is, in fact, as we know, the so-called *homo oeconomicus*, as described for example by Pierre Dardot and Christian Laval: a

competitive, narcissistic and self-entrepreneurial neo-subject. It is from this theoretical perspective that we will analyze in synthesis the psychological constitution of the neoliberal subject. Laclau's hypothesis is based on an Oedipal construction of subjectification based on the interdiction of desire in its deferment, both Kantian and Freudian. In other words, we find ourselves in the midst of the "Oedipal" theorem of modernity. Laclau, therefore, does not grasp the current emergence of a neo-subject dominated by a logic of the *plus-jouir* equal and parallel to the extraction of the *plus-value*, that is, the immediate and mirroring enlargement of jouissance and hyper-production. This temperament determines a process of subjectification that implies the logic of *relying on the leader* on which Laclau's theory is based. In other words, we are faced with an already recognised Oedipal identification with the leader: a failed leader, enslaved and consumed by the media device. In this sense, one could speak of "indebted sovereignty" in the sense of the ghost of impotence that inhabits the virile leadership of the contemporary world. There is, in fact, as already mentioned, an unspoken idea in Laclau's remarks: that is, the concept of *demand* that constitutes the link between populism and the market.

3. Consider the revival of Lacanian psychoanalysis in the reading of today's politics (see, for example, Slavoj Žižek (2009)), especially in the late elaboration of the evaporation of the Father, that is, in the complete failure of the Oedipal device. In the reading of the aforementioned Laclau, in fact, the consubstantiality between populism and liberal democracy is given in the opacity of subjects that are both identical-centric and differentiated. But we will address this aspect later on.

First, in fact, we would like to clarify that approach to populism that derives from the late lecture series by Michel Foucault, and especially from the central course of 1978-79 "Birth of biopolitics": a course in which we see the emergence of the concept of "people", or rather "population", brought back from the end of a discourse born with Hegel, namely the *political economy*. In fact, as we read in the course, the market has not only a power of formalization in relation to both the state and society, but represents, in its neoliberal transformation, an absolutely radical change. It is not simply a question of freeing up the economy, but also of knowing to what extent the political and social powers of information of the market economy can be extended. From this point of view, neoliberalism has brought about a number of shifts and transformations. The first and crucial shift is the one that sees the transition from the principle of exchange to the principle of competition of the market economy. In other words, it is argued that the essence of the market is constituted by competition and therefore not by equality, but on the contrary, by *inequality*. However, in this context we are interested in the impact on the subjects of this transformation. In fact, Foucault writes: "also in neo-liberalism - which does not hide it, but rather proclaims it - one finds a theory of the *homo oeconomicus* which, however, is not understood at all as a partner in the exchange. The *homo oeconomicus* is rather an entrepreneur, he is the entrepreneur of himself. This aspect is so true that practically all the analyses made by neo-liberals will have as their goal the substitution at every point of the *homo oeconomicus* understood as a partner in the exchange, with the *homo oeconomicus* conceived as an entrepreneur of himself, that as such he is his own capital, the producer of himself and the source of his (own) incomes" (2004 page?). To avoid going back to the already mentioned Dardot and Laval, reference should be made to the diagnosis of the *crisis of democracy* in Western countries or, more precisely, to the *processes of de-democratization* drawn up by Wendy Brown in "Neoliberalism and the end of democracy" (2003). The "active" neoliberal policies produce in fact a calculating subject, self-directing, entrepreneur of himself. In other words, it is a constructivist project that sees economic rationality extend into all the domains of existence. This project, which replaces the political and moral normativity which had dominated the liberal democracies, sanctions the *death of the democratic subject* who constituted the ideal reference point of the liberal democracy. In other words, the figure of the citizen disappears in a generalisation of the entrepreneurial form.

4. But let us return to Ernesto Laclau's seminal idea of post-Marxism as formulated in "Socialist Strategy and Hegemony" (1985), written with Chantal Mouffe and already centered on the

Hegelian element of the synthesis of time. In this element resides in fact the catechontic dimension of Laclau's populism. And this is testified by the centrality enjoyed in Laclau as well as in Chantal Mouffe (2005) by an author like Carl Schmitt: Hegel and Schmitt are in fact authors whose thought is centered on the *maintenance of order*. From this genealogy we can thus derive that tension to the reconstruction of order and social totality that can be found in "Populist reason" (Laclau 2005), despite the criticism of the various post-Marxisms, of feminism and of the different theoretical-social movements following the fall of Orthodox Marxism. In short, we are faced with a reconstructive position. In other words, Laclau offers no real alternative to today's capitalist neoliberalism. Let us think, for example, of Laclau's concept of the people. Nowhere, in fact, does Laclau attribute to it a constituent power. Rather, the people present themselves as a continuous process of constitution in the production of a series of equivalent chains that has no end. It is based on a continuous metonymical mechanism that on the one hand makes the concept of nation re-emerge as an alternative to the people, and on the other hand and above all builds the figure of the leader as a catachresis of a dynamic totality in a self-generative process.

Laclau's work does not take into account the fact that the psychological form of neoliberalism is not compatible with democracy. In fact, today's financial capitalism is no longer based on accumulation, but on concentration (Appadurai). In conclusion, what we want to maintain is that the psychological system (sense of self) does not and cannot withstand this capitalism of unlimited concentration and consumption. All this starting from the observation that we find ourselves today in a climate marked by the emergence of a post-oedipal man (Roudinesco). From this point of view, the problem of the death drive becomes central, as it is known to be fundamental in a person's psychological makeup. If financial capitalism is productive of the future (Appadurai), the death instinct itself has notoriously to do with temporalization and with the future. A principle of unlimited pleasure, such as that which characterizes the present post-oedipal man, cannot in fact govern the death drive, but only generate a phantasmal production.

And - this is our thesis - the "ghost" can only produce a helpless leader, unlike the "symbol" which has a function of recomposition. This thesis is also supported by authoritative sociologists. What is missing in Laclau's theory, namely the principle of representation, is also what, according to authoritative political and sociological experts, is lacking in the so-called current "popolocracy": a term by which we mean a form of "immediate democracy", i.e., without mediation, based on characters such as *personalization*, the centrality of the body of the leader (Belpoliti 2011) and above all, as already mentioned, on a mechanism of *identification*.

5. Yet, it is now time to conclude. As we have tried to argue, the current neoliberal capitalist configuration produces "precarious lives" or residual lives that place *trust* without mediation in charismatic figures and tendentially anti-democratic ones. At this time we would like to propose as a temporary alternative the idea of republicanism, i.e., the Roman *res publica* as a flexible institutionalism, or better still, the "city" as the matrix of a new urban and metropolitan federalism. In other words, a new municipalism as not only a link between cities but also as a civilizing system of the economy. To this we want to add the centrality of the body, opposed to the mechanism of incarnation in a leader, as a new perspective of democratization, on the basis of what Judith Butler called a "street policy" and we call a possible "democracy of the bodies". With this we assume not only that the "signifier" of democracy is multi-faceted and the object of an open political struggle, but also that "the people" is a dynamic concept that must remain constantly open to "unexpected guests", to subjects and themes of unpredictable transformation, whose entry on the scene of the democratic struggle can only force us to redefine the whole from time to time.

Bibliography

Appadurai Arjun, (2016), *Banking on Words. The Failure of Language in the Age of Derivative Finance*, University of Chicago Press, Chicago.
AA.VV., (2013), *Qu'est-ce qu'un peuple?*, La Fabrique éditions, Paris.
Balibar Étienne, (2016), *Europe: crise et fin?*, Le Bord de l'eau, Lormont.
Belpoliti Marco, (2011), *Il corpo del capo*, Guanda, Milano.
Brown Wendy, (2003), 'Neo-liberalism and the End of Liberal Democracy', in *Theory and Event*, 7 (1).
Brown Wendy, (2005), *Undoing the Demos: Neoliberalism's Stealth Revolution*, Zone Books, The MIT Press.
Butler Judith-Ernesto Laclau-Slavoj Žižek, (2000), *Contingency, Hegemony, Universality*, Verso, London.
Butler Judith, (2006), *Precarious Life: The Power Of Mourning And Violence*, Verso, London.
Butler Judith, (2013), *Vita buona e vita cattiva: Can One Lead a Good Life in Bad Life?*, nottetempo, Roma.
Butler Judith, (2015), *Notes Toward a Performative Theory of Assembly*, The President and Fellows of Harvard College.
Carandini Andrea, (2007), *Sindrome occidentale*, Il nuovo melangolo, Genova.
Dardot Pierre and Laval Christian, (2009), *La nouvelle raison du monde. Essais sur la société néolibérale*, La découverte, Paris.
Diamanti Ilvo-Lazar Marc, (2018), *Popolocrazia*, Laterza, Bari-Roma.
Fornari Emanuela, (2017), 'La democrazia dei corpi', in *Paradigmi. Rivista di critica filosofica*, n.3.
Foucault Michel, (2004), *Naissance de la biopolitique. Cours au Collège de France 1978-1979*, Seuil, Gallimard.
Laclau Ernesto and Chantal Mouffe, (1985), *Hegemony and Socialist Strategy*, Verso, London.
Laclau Ernesto, (2005), *On Populist Reason*, Verso, London.
Lacan Jacques, (1968), 'Note sur le Père et l'universalisme', in *Le Séminaire. Livre XVI*, Seuil, Paris.

Lefebvre Henri, (1974), *Espace et Politique. Le droit à la ville II*, Paris.

Mouffe Chantal, (2005), *On the Political Reason (Thinking in Action)*, Routledge, New York.

Müller Jan Werner, (2016), *What is populism?*, University of Pennsylvania Press.

Revelli Marco, (2017), *Populismo 2.0*, Einaudi, Torino.

Rosanvallon Pierre,(2006), *La contre-démocratie. La politique à l'âge de la défiance*, Seuil, Paris.

Roudinesco Elisabeth, (2006), *La famiglia in disordine*, Booklet Editore, Milano.

Olgivie Bertrand, (2012), *L'homme Jetable*, Editions Amsterdam, Paris.

Villacañas Berlanga José Luis, (2015), *Populismo*, La Huerta Grande, Madrid.

Žižek Slavoj, (2009), *The Ticklish Subject. The Absent Centre of Political Ontology*, Verso, London.

Jorge Álvarez Yágüez
THE LIMITS OF THE CONCEPT OF HEGEMONY
Gramsci and Laclau-Mouffe

1. *The Long History of a Concept*

In his last book, Perry Anderson makes a historical review of the concept of hegemony[1]. Its origin dates back to Homeric texts, where the term is used as a verb meaning "to guide", "to conduct". As a noun, hegemony first appears in Herodotus, with the meaning of leadership in the context of a military alliance formed by city-states, *poleis*; and very soon this meaning coexisted with the concept of archê, government, coercion by an asserted authority. Both in Herodotus and in Thucydides hegemony and *archê* overlap. Since then, the concept has remained ambiguous, combining leadership and coercion. This double meaning, according to P. Anderson, would have earned him his persistence in very different cultures. The term would have been lost after Greece. The Roman world did not seem to need it in its work of imperial domination. It does not appear in Middle Age. And already in the Modern Age, Hobbes, curiously makes no distinction between hegemony and *archê* when translating to Thucydides. The term hegemony will not be taken up until the middle of the 19th century in the context of the division of the Germanic principalities and the problem of unification, in which historians inspired in Greece attributed to Prussia the potential to lead the unity of the German states, which embodies a *Führung* or *Vorherrschaft*[2]. In the 20th century, the term would be primarily used by Russian social democracy and the Bolsheviks.

---

[1] Anderson P., The H-Word. *The Peripeteia of Hegemony*, London, Verso, 2017.
[2] *Ibid*. pp. 1-11.

2. *Gramsci*

However, the concept only acquires a profound theoretical development with Antonio Gramsci, who used it primarily to understand the system of class domination in societies of developed capitalism and the practical possibility of overcoming it. The concept had a weak presence in the pre-prison writings, and with a meaning very attached to the Leninist conception: the hegemony of the working class over the peasantry, and the performance by the proletariat of tasks that would have corresponded to the bourgeoisie. Just as in the prison writings, the concept acquires a dimension that takes it far beyond the Leninist meaning, as it does not only refer to a particular *strategy*, but to a *system of power*.

The concept of hegemony is the true core of his thought, articulated to a plexus of other relevant concepts such as State, historical block, war of movement, war of position, intellectuals, organic crisis, passive revolution, common sense and good sense, folklore and so on. It would not be possible to enter the Gramscian theory of hegemony without starting up all these and other concepts; The whole conceptual framework of the Quaderni revolves around the category of hegemony.

The concept, on the other hand, was inserted into a philosophical framework that involved a whole critique of economism, of a special philosophy of history, of vulgar materialism, or of the relationship between theory and action. His conception was aptly named *absolute historicism* or *philosophy of praxis*.

3. *Forgetfulness and Return of Gramsci*

Since the *Quaderni* were announced, between 1948 and 1951, the interpretation of the concept of hegemony has gone through very different times. In his own country – and the reception in France and Spain was very similar- the debate was closely linked to the needs and political diagnoses of the situation by the PCI, from the national policy-people of Togliatti to the *compromesso storico* and the euro-communism of Berlinguer.

In contrast to this reading, called "revisionist" or social

democrat, in terms of time, emerged another one that intended to highlight the revolutionary Gramsci, Gramsci of the *consigli di fabbrica* without rupture with the posterior Gramsci, the author of *Quaderni*; which, often, not always, entailed the image of a Leninist Gramsci.

Soon, other readings were added, above all from Britain and North America, considered by Anderson much more creative; for example, the so-called *Culture Studies*, founded by Stuart Hall in Birmingham in 1964, that had a long continuation in the United States of America. Later, the *Subaltern Studies* were added to them, above all in relation to Third World. These new works would maintain the attention about Gramsci until the nineties and beyond (Guha, Spivak).

And when Gramsci seemed, at least in Europe, a figure from another time, a classic somewhat forgotten, he returns, especially with his concept of hegemony, in the context of success of new populist movements, especially in South America, with the so-called " left-wing populism". The thought of Ernesto Laclau has played a relevant role in this return because he attempted to give a new and finest theoretical foundation to populism. That was particularly made in his book *On Populist Reason* (2005). However, it is essential to take into account a previous and important book, written in collaboration with Chantal Mouffe, *Hegemony and Socialist Strategy* (1985)[3], where the authors made a fine criticism of the political theory of the Sardinian thinker.

**

In what follows, firstly, the critique of Gramsci's concept of hegemony by Laclau and Mouffe, whose conception is used by many authors in relation to populism, will be analyzed. Secondly, the problems of this alternative will be raised. And, finally, the current difficulties faced by the concept of Gramsci's hegemony will be pointed out.

---

3   E. Laclau, C. Mouffe, *Hegemony and Socialist Strategy. Towards a Radical Democratic Politics,* London, Verso, 1985 (HS). E. Laclau, *On Populist Reason*, London, Verso, 2005.

4. The Criticism made by Laclau and Mouffe

Perhaps, the most important criticism to Gramsci, after the well-known critique of Althusser in *Lire Le Capital,* (1965), was made by Laclau and Mouffe, a long time after, in 1985, in the aforementioned book *Hegemony and Socialist Strategy*. Laclau and Mouffe, after making a wise genealogy of the concept of hegemony, in which the historian Perry Anderson[4] had preceded them, since its use by the Russian Social Democrats and by Lenin himself, recognize that Gramsci took the concept of hegemony further than anyone else, especially by not reducing it to an assumption of a political program that does not correspond to its direct class interests, or to a strategic alliance, but rather to a whole constitution of a new historical block, in which the cultural dimension, in a broad, moral and intellectual sense, gained enormous relevance; all of this in the context of the attempt to solve the specific problems that the revolution faces in the West compared to the Russian case.

Gramsci, according to Laclau and Mouffe, would have had the merit of displaying a much more complex concept of *ideology*, which was not reduced to a more or less varied set of ideas, nor did it necessarily have the effect of a *false consciousness*. Ideology involves a varied mix of elements; a true set of institutions and devices (the "materiality of ideology", HS. 67), and cannot be strictly placed, as usual, on the superstructure plane. Ideology would fulfill a foundational role of a historical block, a union of base and superstructure, poles which in Gramsci acquire a much more complex and nuanced nature and connection[5].

Laclau and Mouffe admit that the dimension of *contingency* plays a role in the Sardinian author which is more important than in any other previous Marxist theorist, leading them to affirm, controversially, that in Gramsci the political subject is not as much a social class as a "collective man", that is, a social group contingently formed through

---

[4] P. Anderson, *The Antinomies of Antonio Gramsci*, New Left Review, L/100, 1976.

[5] Cfr. Chantal Mouffe, "Hegemony and Ideology in Gramsci", en C. Mouffe (ed.), *Gramsci and Marxist Theory*, London, Routledge, 1979, pp.168-204.

the mechanisms of hegemony, in which class membership would no longer be determinable (HS, 67); the initial identities would be transformed along the hegemonic process. Without a doubt, Gramsci admitted the transformation of the first preferences of social actors, but going beyond this, would imply attributing a radical constructivism difficult to find in his work.

However, from his point of view, Gramsci, in his critical work, did not go far enough. Indeed, although Gramsci would have gone further than anyone in this journey of complexing hegemony, through, among other elements, a new concept of *ideology*, of overcoming a *philosophy of history* determined by the relevant inclusion of *contingency*, of the distancing from *economist* positions, however, could not have saved serious difficulties in its development, which would be synthesized in what these authors call *essentialism*, because, in short, all those bold innovations would be burdened by the maintenance of "dualism of classical Marxism" and the role assigned to the "determination in the last instance by the economy"(HS, 69, 85). That is, for Gramsci, the whole hegemonic process would still move within the framework of the social struggle between the two *fundamental classes* that define a mode of *production*; insofar as social classes are essentially constituted by their place in production, it is the economy that finally sets the limits on the constitution of the "collective man" and the inscription of contingency. Even, in spite of the role given to action by this philosopher of praxis, it would keep what Laclau-Mouffe called "naturalistic prejudice" (HS, 69, 76) or "economist paradigm" (HS, 76).

Gramsci would not unleash his bond with the Marxist tradition while remaining in a "fundamental ambiguity" (HS, 69), which basically revolves around the place granted to the working class, which, on the one hand, is supposed to be historically and contingently shaped in its role as historical subject but, on the other hand, such a role comes in advance assigned by the economic structure (HS, 70). Therefore, the constitution of the subjects, their historical role, their tasks or objectives to which they are oriented are not entirely decided by the hegemonic process in its contingent functions. The extreme contingentism of Laclau and Mouffe separated them, ultimately, from the Gramsci's theory of hegemony.

According to these authors, Gramsci would not have known

how to extract all the deconstructive consequences of the shift to Marxist theory by its concept of hegemony. Otherwise, one would have to admit that the "logic of hegemony, as the logic of articulation and contingency, has come to determine the complete identity of hegemonic subjects" (HS, 85).

As one can see, what Laclau and Mouffe finally raised to Gramsci was excessive. They demanded from the secretary and co-founder of the Italian Communist Party, to break with the keys of Marxist theory, to adopt instead a strict contingentist conception of the historical-political processes, oblivious to the structural determinations, which unlinked its decisive bond with the economy, opening to a different constitution of social identities no longer predefined by the concept of social class.

In the well-known letter to Weidemeyer (March 5, 1852), Marx stated that his theoretical contribution consisted in adding to conception of the class struggle, used by bourgeois historians as Thierry and Guizot, the fact that those social classes were constituted depending on their place in the production in a way that confrontation would lead to the dictatorship of the proletariat. Although Laclau and Mouffe did not mention the Marxian text, what Gramsci would really demand was that in his contingentism, in his struggle against economism, rupture with a linear and gradualist conception of history, he took another step and abandoned everything involved in such a Marxian contribution: the *economic determination*, which was preserved, however attenuated or complexed with other factors of historical intervention; that the same concept of *class struggle* was detached even though Gramsci understood this in relation to a strong political construction of social subjects; and the predefined orientation towards a certain end of such a struggle despite the fact that he insisted so much that it would not occur spontaneously or be imposed in any necessary process, but would require the conscious and active role of self-constructed subjects. The criticisms, which over time, Žižek threw specifically at Laclau, which led to a debate between them, would have much to do with that demanded abandonment of the Marxian keys[6].

---

6 About the debate between Žižek and Laclau: S. Žižek: J. Butler, E. Laclau and S. Žižek, *Contingency, Hegemony, Universality*, London,

If the criticisms made by Althusser and P. Anderson were carried out from Marxist theses and intended a more refined cleansing of aspects of Gramsci's theory in accordance with a certain reading of those theses, the criticism made by Laclau and Mouffe no longer have such an orientation and demand a withdrawal of the so-called economic paradigm that would completely define Marxism. The concept of hegemony, already cleared from the Marxian burden, would still undergo transformations in Laclau´s hands. In a later book, *On Populist Reason*, 2005, an operation started in *Hegemony and Socialist Strategy* ,1985, was prolonged. In this book, the comparison between the concepts of hegemony and politics was proposed and now (in On Populist Reason) the equivalence between politics and populism was made, so that the three concepts: politics, hegemony and populism, overlapped."[7]. The most characteristic features of politics would not be other than those that define populism, and for which it is so criticized: antagonistic dichotomization, constitution of a broad subject, people, through the mechanism called "chain of equivalences" between demands not absorbed by the institutions, identification by means of generic discourses, use of empty signifiers, with an outstanding affective load, relevant role of the leader as a means of unification of a totality only suturable in the imaginary. Populism, therefore, is essentially politics itself. Anyone who wants to know about it has its best exposure in it. For this reason, Laclau did not understand populism as an ideology but in a formal way, as a set of resources, as a style.

If hegemony consisted of the same political game, and this is

Verso, 2000; S. Žižek, "Against the Populist Temptation", *Critical Inquiry* 32, Spring 2006, pp. 551-574; S. Žižek, "Schlagend, aber nicht Treffend!", *Critical Inquiry* 33, Autumn, 2006, pp. 185-211. E. Laclau; "Por qué construir un pueblo es la tarea principal de la política radical", *Cuadernos del CENDES*, 23, 62, mayo-agosto 2006, pp. 1-36; E. Laclau, *On Popullist Reason* op. cit, pp. 232-244.

7   These were the final words of *Hegemony and Socialist Strategy*: "The field of the political as the space for a game which is never zero-sum, because the rules and the players are never fully explicit. This game, which eludes the concept, does at least have a name: hegemony" (HS, 193). In *On Populist Reason* it was said: "That is why populist reason -which amounts, as we have seen, to political reason tout court", op. cit, p. 225.

nothing but populism, hegemony would be the game of populism. And if Gramsci was at the base of a category, it would have to be consistent and put it in relevant relationship with the other. That is what is seen in the defenders of populism when they use the device of Gramsci for their political strategy. Thus, in this particular way, Gramsci returns. But our goal is not to criticize this theory of populism, but to examine the concept of hegemony of Laclau and Mouffe in confrontation with its Gramscian origin. The concept undergoes three significant reductions:

1) *Constructivism and Contingentism*. The most obvious reduction, but also with an interesting content that could take on other approaches, is linked to the location of hegemony in a post-Marxist framework: the concept, as the core strategy defined as war of position, or of a historical block or system of power, would be deprived of its articulation to what we call central elements of the Marxian theory: division of society into two antagonistic classes defined by the place they have in production; ultimate economic determination of the process of historical development of the struggle between the two classes; approaching that process to a new mode of production. The constructivism ex nihilo and extreme contingentism of Laclau-Mouffe go very far by this way, because it is not only a certain teleological, mechanistic and economist conception of Marxism that is put in question here, a critic in Gramsci had stood out more than anyone, but the same idea of social class, going beyond what the social sciences allow, since this has problematized them, pointed out their blurred contours, highlighted, in their identity, the less economic elements, emphasizing their fragmentation and progressive multiplicity, but they have not concluded much less to declare their liquidation or inoperance.

The same should be said about the influence of the structures to which the practices, otherwise eminently discursive, would seem alien. To all that should be added, the power of *economic determination* that the current phase of capitalist development has acquired, that of the dominance of financial capital framed by neoliberal conceptions.

2) *Discursivity and Equivalences*. A second thinning of the concept of hegemony is of a *cultural nature*. In Gramsci this dimension of hegemony, was certainly central, and was in

relationship with many other concepts mentioned as intellectual, common sense, folklore, worldview, organic crisis, passive revolution, etc. This dimension was essential both in terms of the *strategy* for the constitution of a class in the ruling class, and prepares it for the government before the seizure of power, as regards to the *system of domination*, because it has a role of union of the social body, so that when it fails only the resource of repression remains, that of coercive power.

Certainly, hegemony is not reduced to a cultural factor, as it includes the *economic*, not only in the aspect included in the expression of "l'egemonia nasce dalla fabrica"[8], but also in the one related to the overcoming of corporatism, of the assumption of others economic demands of other classes; Gramsci called it *"economica"* hegemony (Q, III, 13, 1591). For this reason, the concepts of ideology, culture and hegemony cannot be overlaid.

In any case, the constitution of the hegemonic subject, according to Laclau, does not go through this long cultural process of emergence of new intellectuals or separation of the service of many of the existing ones to the class in power, as by the establishment of the aforementioned *chain of equivalences*, the main hegemonic mechanism, which is essentially obtained through an eminently discursive process in which the notions of *floating signifier* and *empty signifier* play a primary role, together with the role of the leader. But all this leaves hegemony in a place almost equivalent to that of the constitution of an electoral majority.

3) *Anormativity*. Finally, an essential dimension of the Gramscian concept of hegemony would be abolished: its pedagogic function. All hegemony entails a particular pedagogy, values, habits and practices, some kind of relationship between elites and the masses, intellectuals and ordinary people. Not all hegemony has the same content, but more importantly, not all hegemony builds the same subjects and subjectivities.

For Gramsci the proletarian hegemony should be very different from the bourgeois hegemony, it should follow the republican principle to form autonomous individuals, free citizens within an autonomous community, therefore the acquired relevance of a

---

8   A. Gramsci, *Quaderni del carcere*, Torino, Einaudi, 1975, III, 22, 2146 (Q).

determined type of revolutionary party and its special relationship with people. This is where the link between the first Gramsci of the *consegli di fabrica* and the second of the *Quaderni* is stronger than any other. And, it is exactly at this point, where the contrast between the type of hegemony that Gramsci was trying to boost and populist hegemony could not be more distant. All the heteronomy that entails the populist emphasis on empty signifiers, emotions, the role of the leader, cannot be more contrary to the pedagogy of the alternation of teacher and disciple that we find developed in the *Quaderni* (Q, II, 10, 1330-1332).

Nothing is more alien to him than that non-place of truth, of the function of *parrhesia* that characterizes populist hegemony in Laclau – let us remember the motto of the group of *L'Ordine Nuovo:* "la verità è semper rivoluzionaria"[9]. Nothing more alien to Gramsci than the instrumental logic of the formulation of Laclau, nothing more alien than the deep instrumentalism in this regard, because finally, the constitution of one signifier or another, is decided not according to any regulations, not in its connection with any truth, this does not require of the burden of proof, but only for that contribution to the designed antagonism, of Schmittian nature, for its contribution to the emergence of the subject People.

It is not necessary to say that these three reductions (constructivism, discursivity and anormativity) are related to each other. From our point of view, the last two reductions are not acceptable; only some aspects of the first could be accepted. Laclau and Mouffe are right when criticising the aspects of *philosophy of history* in Marxism and what still remains of it in Gramsci and also in regard to the idea of the existence of a *privileged class*, or of the *dualism* in the class struggle. But it is already more difficult to admit the equalization of the different instances (economic, ideological, social, political) within the historic determination. It would be very distinct if speaking about conjunctural situations, as Marx himself did in his historical and political writings.

There are two important points that Laclau overlooks, and they should be critically considered:

---

[9] Cf. A. Gramsci, *Quaderni...* op. cit, I, 6 pp. 699-700.

a) The relation of subordination between the principal social group, the group that, according to Laclau, represents the universal, the *plebs* that appear as the *people*. This part will put in second place the interests of other groups, which adopt, then, a subordinate position. The assumption that the leading party makes, of the will of other groups, is always tactical, in function of consolidating its own position of power. That way, the effects, certainly criticizable, of a historical privileged subject is reproduced in this part denominated as *plebs*. It is true that the hegemonic totality, the relation between particular and universal is not suturable because the demands maintain the differences in spite of the chain of equivalences, and the part never can represent the whole. However, the totality is closed, sutured in the imaginary, symbolically, through the power of discourse and the figure of the leader; and this real totality will be coercive against the differences.

b) The dimension of coercion is present also in all kind of hegemony, like it was always since the Greek origin of this concept. Gramsci certainly made emphasis on the persuasive dimension of hegemony, on the side of consensus, but this aspect was always jointed to the side of coercion; the difference was only *analytic*. Both dimensions formed part of the same phenomenon. The coercive dimension does not disappear, even in institutions that would apparently realize only functions of consensus or direction; for example, in the case of school, where it exists in the form of watching and sanctions, or in the case of the political party organized according to the model of State, or even, curiously, inside the individual himself, whose reason has to *educate* the sentiments but also to *dominate* the instincts. Without a doubt, this side would have to be subdued to control and criticism, but this point is not problematized by Laclau and Mouffe.

5. The Future of the Gramscian Concept

5.1 *State, State-Nation and Form-State*

The whole operation of hegemony is delimited on the concept of State. It is well-known that the modification of the State's concept that was made by Gramsci through the formulation: "Stato =

società politica + società civile" (Q, II, 6, 763-764). This point was the key to explain the difficulties for the revolution in Western. In Russia, however, the State had not this complexity, there "lo Stato era tutto, la socità civile era primordiale e gelatinosa" (Q, II, 7, 866). The hegemony in Western was more solid, a device that generates consensus and not only coercion, that is placed in a second place. The strategy of war of position was a consequence of this difference.

The erosion of the existent hegemony should go simultaneously with the construction of a new hegemony that would set a national-popular block. According to Gramsci, the contra hegemonic block would have to build step by step its own state, or, as he said, the working class should become state; it would have to be leading class before to be formally ruling class, with the capacity, then, to articulate and to guide the whole society. The alternative movement would be cut according to the state pattern, And Gramsci does not forget the coercive functions, essential for that. The new Prince, the political party, vanguard of the working class would be organized in the same way, according to the state model. This is the form of the whole process.

Gramsci operated in a context in which the centrality of state apparatus in a framework of conflict among nations was unquestionable. But, certainly, our situation is other, defined by global interdependence in which new international subjects intervene in addition to state, and the powers of this state are limited up and down, sharing its idealized sovereignty with other international and local entities.

Today is not possible to return to the concept of Vanguard-Party, a kind of anticipate state, not less centralized, capable to determine the whole society

5.2 *Ideological Totalization*

The ideology is an essential element of the concept of hegemony due to the main cultural dimension of this. We have already alluded to it. It is known that this concept in Gramsci has a different meaning than in Marx because it is not the opposite of science, and it not always has a deceptive dimension, it does not necessarily represent false consciousness; it is in connection with the Marxian original idea about people taking consciousness of social conflicts through ideology[10]. The ideology covers a wide field not reducible to ideas because it comprehends also a heterogeneous set of practical elements, habits, affections, etc. On the other hand, ideology crosses the whole field of economy, as the Gramscian studies on the denominated "Americanism" show. In spite of these relevant contributions, this concept was entirely affected by its *totalizing* character. It involves always a kind of *Weltanschauung* that is in relationship with the two main class in struggle. That way, the strategy of conformation of an alternative hegemony in regard to bourgeois hegemony would acquire similar totalisation, but expressive of another worldview. The problem is that the complexity of current societies avoids these totalizing processes, it prevents that the whole is folded to a closed worldview.

5.3 The Polemical Role of Culture

In regard of the important role attributed by Gramsci to cultural and ideological factor, it should be questioned if this, indeed, is the main factor in the construction of hegemony in the current capitalist societies and if this is the factor that holds society together . We would like to raise three aspects that would question this:

1) First, the fact that these societies generate also its own self-criticism due to several processes and mechanisms: the characteristic of social conflict, with its effects of cognitive dissonance; the individualization; the increasing levels of formation; the known autonomization of spheres of action (Weber); the rationalization of the *Lebenswelt* (Habermas). All this contributes to a less cloudy view of the social reality and neutralizes the possible univocal and integrating effect of the cultural instance.

2) Second, in the same way, it operates the Marxian formulation of "The anatomy of man is a key to the anatomy of the ape"[11],

---

10   K. Marx, Preface to *Contribution to Critique of Political Economy,* Marx, Engels, *Collected Works,* vol. 29, New York, International Publisher, 1985, p. 263.

11   K. Marx, "Introduction" to *Economic Manuscripts of 1857-61* [Grundrisse], Marx, Engels, *Collected Works,* vol. 29, op. cit, p. 42.

that is, the anatomy of the system is revealed through its high development.

3) The normal situation in our societies is more like the denominated "passive hegemony" (Gramsci) or "unbelieving faith in the existence" (Horkheimer), that is, a resigned acquiescence to the given. The mechanisms of integration do not operate through the consciousness; are not-discursive mechanisms, but simple functioning, or effects derived of costs of action, and depending on networks of social dependency; or also devices similar to disciplines, studied by Weber and Foucault, with its effects of *assujettissement* (subjection), that mark the behavior of agents without consensus or violence; that constitute the own individuality. In this line were the studies of Gramsci about the Americanism or Fordism, about the psycho-physical adaption of the worker. Of course, it should be mentioned that these mechanisms studied by Freudo-Marxism in relation with psychic apparat, the libidinal structure, the pseudo-necessities, etc. All of them have as an effect, a continuous adjustment of the individual to the existent order. Marx named this "real subsumption of labour under capital"[12].

6. *Hegemony and Posthegemony*

The concept of hegemony would certainly have to be refined from many of the elements already critically annotated, as vanguard working class in history, as dictatorship of the proletariat, as teleology in regard to Communism, but also, the centrality of form-State, the idea of political party, the ideology as totalizing conception, the virtual use of violence as a political tool, the instrumental logic in regard to relations among political subjects, the imposed subalternity, and effectively the totalizing dimension. But what would leave after these depurations?

The capacity of self-government of a society is an essential value, of course; and no objection would be made to its conversion

---

12   *Economic Manuscripts 1861-63*, Marx, Engels, *Collected Works*, vol 34, op. cit, p. 93.

in a hegemonic value. That is, there will always be something that demands the hegemony for establishing an order. However, if the great difficulty lies in the *totalizing*, when it acquires substantiality and becomes potentially coercive, then only the established as hegemonic can have a *formal* nature and that would not only be incompatible with the plurality but it could be its own guarantee. The hegemony we are speaking about here would be about the conditions of possibility of the political, of the democracy, what is above all *form* and where nothing is materially (in regard to the content) determined at the beginning. Certainly, all this involves a set of material conditions in relationship with the formation of citizens and its resources for their plural life projects. The necessary conquest of these conditions can only happen in a relationship of reciprocity between form and what it involves, so that in the process of institutionalization of a form its materiality could be solved, and this favors the definition of the form. In that consists, by the way, the *autonomous* dimension of the political itself, its inevitable circularity.

The attempt, logically legitimate, to make a material claim becoming hegemonic cannot enter into conflict with the form. This marks the limits. On the other hand, these claims shall maintain always the plurality due to the differences of individuals, groups, classes and the inherent conflict of modern societies. Everyone will have its representative and it would be impossible to reduce to the unity. These always partial hegemonies can be articulated during a large historic process and someone could perceive later some kind of conception of the world in it, a kind of ideology of epoch, would be a consequence not anticipated by any plan. In this case, only in a retrospective time, it would be possible to speak of a material and formal hegemony.

A hegemony of this type, far from representing a danger of closure and coercion, would be an active support for the new order, in that way the law would be accepted not due to the threat that it represents, but to the fact that the citizens share its values; and in case of dissent, they would refer to the same principles in order to justify its position. According to that, hegemony and republicanism could walk together.

In the same sense, hegemony, as opposed to coercion, could be maintained as a type of political strategy that, within the mentioned conditions, tries to mark a direction, not a plan but a principle of action (Arendt) that the movement itself and its interactions would go modifying as well as the subjects. A strategy characterized by the persuasion, deliberation, as a cultural movement, in a wide sense, and therefore less instrumentalist. Here the pedagogic dimension would appoint a horizontal relationship between senders (organizations, parties, intellectuals) and receivers, a dialogical relationship in which the positions of teacher and disciple are interchangeable. It would continue being part of this strategy the achievement of the capacity of self-government before coming to power.

We think that is what could be preserved from the Gramscian concept in a context whose nature is already *posthegemonic*. A context that resists to the old model of hegemony because this new context hinders structurally all mechanism of suture, still present in the Gramscian conception. These mechanisms are not only not viable but they also lack all normative potential. In this post hegemonic horizon, plurality, *poliarchê, concordia discors* and conflict shall always be significant elements of any authentic alternative.

SECTION 2

THE SUBJECTS AT THE TIME OF POSTDEMOCRACY

Roberto Esposito
POST-DEMOCRACY AND BIOPOLITICS

We only started talking about "post-democracy" from the beginning of this new century. This thesis can be confirmed by the title of Colin Crouch's book (2003) from 2000, while the interview with Dahrendorf, entitled "After Democracy" (2001), is from the following year. The thesis argued by both authors is that, as long as the formal institutions of democracy remain alive, its living substance is exhausted in favor of a different regime that can no longer be properly called "democratic". Both identify the causes of this shift with a triple crisis – of representation, legitimacy and sovereignty – that is in turn dependent on the dynamics of globalization which, in the last thirty years, have undermined the foundations of the very site of modern democracy, that is to say, the Nation-States in which it was born and developed. On the one hand, this has led to a shift of power towards supranational economic-financial organizations that are not elected, and are therefore democratically illegitimate. On the other hand, the vertical crisis of mediating bodies – such as parties, trade unions, and parliaments themselves – in favor of a growing personalization of politics, which is both cause and effect of that populist tendency underway in Europe as well as in America, and which has become the main target of the entire establishment and its mediating organs.

Is this reconstruction convincing? Does it characterize the real extent of the ongoing crisis? I am not at all convinced. Not so much because the phenomenology itself is wrong, but because those who try to think contemporary events in genealogical terms simplify and reduce a much longer and more complex story into a span of twenty years. It is not possible here to trace a rapid profile of this profound history, stopping at some salient moments, all of which can be traced back to a process of governmentality of social life, defined by Foucault with the term, in truth today rather abused, of " biopolitics "(Foucault, 2005).

The first moment of this path, naturally bumpy and contradictory as are all long-term historical processes, can be found at the beginning of the eighteenth century. At this point, the life of the population ceases to be considered by the sovereign as a resource to be consumed, even as cannon fodder, and becomes a valuable asset that requires protection and development. It is then, with the progressive transformation of the sovereign regime into a governmental regime, that the first devices for controlling and regulating collective life are born and developed, activated first by pastoral power and then by so-called police knowledge, together with the establishment of health and social public services.

The second event, perhaps even more crucial in the relationship between power and knowledge, is constituted by the birth of biology as an autonomous discipline at the beginning of the nineteenth century. It is then that the biological life of individuals and populations begins to become a specialized and performative knowledge, of which the most representative names are Bichat, Couvier, Lamarck and Darwin. What are the consequences of the birth and development of biological knowledge for the forms of politics, when one of the objectives of power is to facilitate the preservation of life and the horizon of history is put into relation with that of nature? It is at this moment when the human species comes into contact with other living species that the human being is first considered, not only as an individual, but also as a member of the species.

At this moment begins a process of progressive desubjectivation began, that is to say a crisis of political subjectivity, with the consequence of dissolving political action itself. The individual, which had always been considered by modern political philosophy, as a subject guided by reason and will is now perceived as a living being traversed and often determined not only by vital needs, but also by irrational instincts and forces rooted in an original biological milieu that goes beyond and often collides with the life of relationships. What would be put into debate is the very presupposition of modern Hobbesian political philosophy, which posits the negation of the natural state as a condition for the birth of the political state. Once one is unable to abstract from his body and from the deep mechanisms that regulate it, the political state and the natural state become inextricably intertwined. This has profound consequences for the way we understand political action. If the human passions are determined in large part by unconscious impulses arising from the depths of organic life, then it will no longer be possible to channel these passions into the geometries of the social contract, of which human subjects can no longer be considered the only authors.

That which begins to be called into question is the compact nucleus of reason and will, attributed to the juridical person, which until then had been considered the constitutive essence of the political subject. At the moment in which the idea of political institutions entirely governed by rational motives weakens, the still young paradigm of democracy also enters into a zone of progressive erosion. It is as if, from then on, the *kratos* of democracy should no longer refer to the *demos*, but rather to a *bios*, if not also to a *ghenos*. In order to give a sense of the transition in progress, I recall three emblematic events that have radically changed the landscape to which we were accustomed. In the late 1960s of the last century the question of gender, generation and genetics always assumes *ghenos* into the democratic *nomos*. Gender, understood as sexual difference, and generation, understood as a set of socio-cultural characteristics, becomes increasingly central. A few years later, the first experiments in genetic manipulation – starting from that of Dolly the sheep – prefigure, at least at the level of possibility, an even closer relationship, however problematic, between human life and technology. Finally, in 1972, the first conference on the environment was held in Stockholm, also making ecology a major political issue.

These events outline a complex paradigm shift: the lives of men, the life of the species, and life in the world enter forcefully into a political scenario unprepared to fully understand their meaning. To believe that a series of changes of this nature, with the question of *bios* and *ghenos* at the center, would leave the political scenario unaltered, was an illusion destined to be continually negated. We can say that since then, in successive waves, our time has been characterized ever more clearly by the breaking of the boundaries between the biological and the political. Since then the questions of life and death, sexuality and public health, migration and security have forcefully entered all political agendas, affecting them widely. Following this transition, the political horizon in turn becomes broader and more complex, expanding and deforming. It is as if the entire modern lexicon, which had shaped politics for more than three centuries, had lost its meaning and crashed under the pressure of events that it is no longer able to represent. Since that time, and indeed for longer than twenty years, the semantics of democracy have become increasingly difficult.

The consequences are easily understood and are now visible to everyone. How are we to employ the democratic lexicon of formal equality between autonomous political subjects when what increasingly matters is the ethnic, sexual, religious differences of human groups defined by the characteristics of their bodies, their age, their sex? Since then it is evident that the old European categories, which had provided the semantic and hermeneutical schema of the twentieth century, no longer work and have begun to turn hollow. The transformation concerns not only democracy, but also classical liberalism, which had forged a century-long alliance. Even liberalism, which is also built on the vocabulary of the individual understood as a subject pursuing his own personal interest in a free market, enters into an even closer relationship with the horizon of life. As Massimo De Carolis (2017) has recently argued, neoliberalism captures the sense of this anthropological and even cosmological turn, expressing at once its potential and its contradictions.

The Austrian neoliberalism of Hayek and Mises (see Ocone 2015) already fuses the market and material life in the same paradigm, literally designing a new "politics of life". But it is above all German ordoliberalism, the group of intellectuals gathered around the magazine *Ordo*, that pushes itself against biopolitical semantics, as Foucault was among the first to indicate, recognizing the novelty and internal antinomies of this process – above all that of producing freedom through its very limitation. Because if one reads books like *Civitas Humana* by Wilhelm Röpke (2017) and *Human Action* by von Mises (2015), then one will see that what results is not just an economic policy, but an anthropological transition which has at its center an intensely biopolitical government of life, not unlike the one otherwise analyzed by Gramsci in *Americanism and Fordism*. Like politics, the economy itself gives value to the human body and the psychology of workers.

Already Rüstow's 1945 essay on the failure of liberalism as a religion (2001) provides for the overcoming of the traditional *laissez faire* in favor of a new social interventionism that penetrates into the very fibers of society. The current German ideology, its obsession with organization, its phobia of the risk of indebtedness, of social conflict, of chaos, was born of ordoliberal culture during those years. What these thinkers imagine is a kind of oxymoron – that is, a social market economy, different from both the Keynesian and the unregulated market. Here the market itself is assumed as a generator of social order. Meanwhile, the State has the task of stabilizing the power of capital by juridical means – but precisely the State not as sovereign, but as government; government of life, religion of work, idolatry of order. The novelty, compared to classical liberalism, of both the Austro-American and the Freiburg School branches of neoliberalism lies in the fact that it explicitly works on the potential of human nature in an anthropological dimension different from the political-state dimension. Its intention is rather to condition human nature by optimizing the natural and vital capacities of man.

We can see how contradictory this project was with respect to the very premise of freeing the market from institutional constraints by the insoluble problems it has encountered from time to time, even in the last economic crisis. Brexit, beyond the most ideological themes, arises from this divergence of the two liberalisms—the Anglo-American and the German. This does not mean that in the end they both fall into the same governmental regime. What unites them is the biopolitical tendency to govern the state of nature, including human nature, rather than abandoning it in favor of the political state, as required by the Hobbesian paradigm. In this sense we can indeed say that we have entered a horizon that Giacomo Marramao (2013) has aptly defined as «post-Leviathanic.»

This also explains the increasingly clear divide between liberalism and democracy that characterizes contemporary Western societies. While democracy remains anchored to the political lexicon of sovereignty, representation, and law, neoliberalism turns toward, albeit in a contradictory fashion, the political lexicon of government, life, and norms. In this sense, neoliberalism is more advanced, from the categorical perspective, than democracy precisely because it has long assumed the biopolitical horizon that democracy still finds difficult to recognize as its own. The cost of this anthropological turn is that the model which carries it out ends up by rendering it inoperative in facing those dynamics that are superficially gathered under the heading of populism and that instead are nothing but the refraction of the politics of the centrality assumed by the dimension of life. This is what radically transforms democratic procedures into the regime that has been given the name of post-democracy.

This touches once again on the profound connection between power and knowledge. How to imagine, for example, an informed consent, necessary for the democratic expression of the vote, in a situation in which the media are in the hands of a few entrepreneurs aimed at protecting their own interests? And how to orient oneself through democratic procedures towards complex problems such as energy sources or the boundaries of human life that even expert commissions cannot answer? Thinking of solving problems of this kind with acts by the parliamentary majority is both impossible and inadequate insofar as the distinctions between public and private, artifice and nature, politics and economics, upon which the democratic conception was formed, have collapsed. When the new statute of the body causes the abstract subjectivity of the juridical person to explode, it becomes difficult to distinguish that which concerns the public sphere from that which belongs to the private sphere, technology from nature, law from theology. Birth and death, sexual life and generational life, health and disease become the faults along which the dams built by modern culture break, giving rise to a radically new political phenomenology.

All three constituent categories of democracy – that is, the electors' representation by the elected, the identity between governors and the governed, and the sovereignty of the people – acquire a very different meaning from what they once had. If sovereignty becomes governmentality, representation becomes simply 're-presentation', understood in a theatrical sense, or better, as television. This in turn transforms the concept of the public, as the opposite of the private, into 'the public' of a media 're-presentation' that is always on the air, even through the connection of the network. A 'public' not only given, but built by polls and referendums whose answers are already prefigured in the questions. The identity between the governed and the governors – as a limit-point of direct democracy – has become an imaginary identification between leader and people, with a consequent loss of boundaries between the symbolic and the real, both oriented by a mimetic desire addressed to the same objects.

The problem we face today is not that of the limits or defects of democracy, but rather of its fulfillment in the figure of its opposite. Does this mean that we must simply confirm the end of democracy or even facilitate it? That we must erase this ancient word, full of history and destiny? This is not what I mean. But we must be aware that our horizon has changed profoundly and irreversibly. At this point a simple reform of democratic institutions is no longer at stake, but rather a deeper socio-cultural shift that involves our entire political language. Far from opposing the new importance assumed by biological life, with the illusion of restoring our 'ancient' modern vocabulary, we must place it ourselves at the center of political action – responding adequately to the pressing demands that come from it, to the dilemmas that it opens, to the needs that continue to lead to ever-larger masses of men and women in the West and its borders.

It would not make sense here to try to compile a list of prescriptions. But something general can be said. Today the language of the left – at least of the European left – is absolutely exhausted, as evidenced by the rapid disappearance of its historical parties. On this point we must be both radical and rigorous – first of all with ourselves. Something of our own way of working, of expressing ourselves, of thinking needs to be changed. We need a shift in our political language appropriate to the transformation we are witnessing. The deconstruction of the Western political lexicon was a demand whose urgency we all felt and that we all tried to implement in different ways. Now this work has been accomplished – in reality, even prior to to our taking on the task. Today the hegemonic language of the modern tradition, with all its errors and violence, with all its imperialisms and colonialisms, is completely in pieces. Rather than continuing to deconstruct what is already abundantly deconstructed, it is a question of trying to construct a new political language, but within the horizon that already surrounds us – that one which is defined by the irreversible centrality of individual and collective life. It is within this horizon that a new political subjectivity and also a new, open and relational principle of identity must be reconstructed. Because differences have a prominence and a meaning [*senso*], they must be thought of together *with* identities, not as an alternative to them. Only identities, recognizable as such, may differ from one another. Of course not all situations are the same. Not all worlds have the same problems. Latin America is experiencing a very different stage from ours, as are North Africa and Southeast Asia. The world is now divided into geopolitical areas whose multiplicity must be defended in a multipolar perspective. In this sense, in order to define their difference, they need to establish their own identity. Among these large spaces we need to build a new balance with respect to the one imposed by a globalization that unifies the world by dividing it between the drowned and the rescued. This means moving a huge mass of vital resources – economic, medical, and ecological – from the West to the Global South. Only in this way will speaking of human rights not sound derisory towards open wounds from old and new colonialisms.

Today, Europe must assume its historical responsibilities and play a decisive role – not only with regard to the dutiful reception of war refugees, but also to support development policies in countries most affected by war, hunger and disease. But, in order to do so, it must first exist as a political subject – to acquire a political subjectivity that at the moment is completely lacking (Esposito, 2016). Europe's deficit of political subjectivity is a problem not only for its countries, but for the whole world. The battle over Europe has a global significance today. Europe urgently needs to be redefined in open but politically realistic terms. The time for dissolution is now behind us. It is a question of rebuilding a more just, more balanced, more generous Europe, because it is aware of itself – of a past full of errors, but also of extraordinary wealth. To get it moving again and transform it at the same time, we need to experience its current crisis as an extreme opportunity to relaunch its role in a world increasingly devoid of reference points.

Translated by Humberto José González Núñez[1]

Bibliography

Crouch C. (2003). *Postdemocrazia*. Roma-Bari: Laterza.
Dahrendorf R. (2001). *Dopo la democrazia*, a cura di A. Polito. Roma-Bari: Laterza.
De Carolis M. (2017). *Il rovescio della libertà*. Macerata: Quodlibet.
Esposito R. (2016). *Da fuori. Una filosofia per l'Europa*. Roma: Einaudi.
Foucault M. (2005). *Nascita della biopolitica*. Milano: Feltrinelli.
Marramao G. (2000, 2013). *Dopo il Leviatano*. Torino: Bollati Boringhieri.
Ocone C. (2015). *Il liberalismo nel Novecento*. Soveria Mannelli: Rubbettino.
Mannelli W. (2015). *Civitas umana*. Soveria Mannelli: Rubbettino.
Mises R. von (2015). *L'azione umana*. Soveria Mannelli: Rubbettino.
Rüstow A. (2001). *Das Versagen des Wirtschaftsliberalismus als religionsgeschichtliches Problem*. Marburg: Metropolis.

Gerardo Muñoz

NOT-ALL DEMOCRACY
Posthegemony and the Crisis of Constitutionalism

> For whom here does the word "liberal" have a meaning? I am a liberal, like everyone else, only in so far as I am anti-progressive…I am caught in a which deserves to be called progressive, for it is progressive to see the discourse of psychoanalysis achieve its foundation insofar as it completes the circle that might perhaps allow you to situate what precisely is at stake…
>
> Jacques Lacan, *Television* (1974)

Can constitutionalism produce a democratic breakthrough in times of the waning of modern sovereignty? This essay departs from the conviction that we are currently living in the ruins of hegemony, understood as the orienting principle of modern political thought as well as the ground for constituent sovereign legitimation. To the extent that legitimacy is integral to constitutional designs, I want to advance a posthegemonic model as one way to think democratic reinvention. If the trending populist experiments around the globe teach us anything, it is that appealing to the notion of "hegemony", in the wake of Ernesto Laclau's important theorization, has ceased to be an efficient response to transform neoliberal domination and the growing depolitization of society. Of course, Laclau's theory of hegemony is already an attempt to respond to the crisis of inter-state hegemony and the Marxist horizon constituted by class antagonism. My hypothesis here is that even the second hegemony cannot be a salient alternative. If liberalism and reactive politics are displaced, one must do more than traverse the myth of political theology or reenact the critique of political economy. Rather, a posthegemonic democracy is what needs to be thought in order to challenge the current transformations of juridical rationalities, subjective processes, and legal developments.

From these premises, the question of constitutionalism has never been more pressing, in spite of the systematic disregard for institutional thinking in contemporary political thought. The organization of this essay will consist of three different movements. First, I want to draw attention to the internal crisis of legal legitimacy in the United States. Secondly, I will move to an example of militant political legality by focusing on the work of legal scholar Kris Kobach. Lastly, I will draw the contours of my larger thesis on posthegemonic democracy as to suggest a passage beyond the closure of the political.

1. *The American crisis of legitimacy*

There is little doubt that there is an ongoing crisis of American constitutionalism. The aftermath of the attacks of 9/11 led to several transformative acts, such as the enactment of the Patriot Act and the boundless statuary power of the Office of Legal Council, which have effectively undermined the separation of powers in conjunction with the menacing rise of the emergency securitarian state (Ackerman, 2010, pp. 87-116). For many liberal constitutionalists, the effective executive power as a re-ordering of internal national security has been an expression and consequence of the making of a strong executive, at times referred as imperial presidency. Although popularized by historian Arthur Schlesinger Jr. during the Nixon presidency, the imperial presidency has been the dominant liberal diagnosis for the rising threat within the constitutional republic (Schlesinger, 1974). Presidential illegitimacy is expressed today thoroughly in a set of concrete practices, such as executive orders, unilateral declarations of wars against non-existent formal war enemies, or "rubber stamping" by NSC lawyers without congressional consent. As constitutionalist Bruce Ackerman told me in an interview I conducted with him at the beginning of last year: «With the new president, Donald J. Trump, what we are really going to see is if the Constitution will survive the next four years» (Muñoz, 2017). For others intellectual observers, the Trump presidency is a symptom in American political life that is only comparable to the constitutional crisis of the Weimar Republic of the 1930s in its depreciation of truth, the rule of law, and institutional boundaries.

Although these diagnoses have many truths in them, it is also the case that they are instances of what Eric Posner and Adrian Vermeule have termed "tyranophobia", which emphasizes the rise of presidentialism in vacuum (Vermeule and Posner, 2009, pp. 176-206). In reality, the potential rise of a tyrant in the American politico-legal context would be almost entirely impossible since the expansion of the presidential reach is symmetrical to the expansion of its internal restraints. Presidentialism is not the most threatening menace of the constitutional crisis, and I would like to suggest that there are two other internal tracks that are more worrisome, to the extent that they pose more durable legal and political effects. I call them internal, because they emerge from within the development of American law over the long twentieth century. Both have fundamental implications for democratic life today.

The crisis of American legitimacy coincides with the rise of the administrative state, or rather, the exceeding power of governmental agencies. The expansion of administrative authority over other branches of governments shatters illusions and assumptions about the separation of powers. Philip Hamburger in his book *Is Administrate Law Unlawful?* (2014), for instance, argues that the juridical and executive delegations to Federal Agencies are unconstitutional under the principle of separation of powers and the illegality lies in a deferred delegation of power (undermining the common law principle *delegate potestas non potesta delegari*). Although some have argued that the administrative state has been a long process of the American legal tradition, its centrality has undertaken a more controversial tone after the watershed case *Chevron vs. NRDC* (1984), in which the Burger Court inaugurated the so-called principle of "deference". Deference means that whenever there is an ambiguous interpretation of a regulatory statue, the case is deferred to agencies and not the courts. This does not mean that courts will always rule in favor of agencies. Rather, it entails that deference will always take place as a preceding principle. However, the most important consequence is that courts then granted administrative agencies a broad statutory discretion to enact, rationalize, interpret, allocate, and execute specific norms and facts under highly arbitrary contexts of decision-making on a broad set and areas of knowledge that affect the common good. The triumph of the administrative state over all spheres of public regulation and everyday planning is an assault on the Jeffersonian tradition of democracy, which sought to lessen the centralization of power among a large federalist arrangement. For good reasons, some theorists have called this "Tocqueville's nightmare" (Ernst, 2016). If what Tocqueville admired in American Democracy was its communitarian and free association patchwork, the new "heart" of law's integrity in America since the New Deal has rested on a bulky administrative state. A counterpoint to this interpretation, however, is that from an internal perspective, the expansion of the administrative state is consistent with development of law's integrity to abandon the centrality of courts and judges. Given the highly rationalized grounds of deference, it is hard to name what aspect of administration breaks away from the law's integrity. According to Adrian Vermeule, the administrative state only signals a natural process of abnegation. Vermeule's thesis argues that:

> [...] law has abdicated its imperial pretension, and has done so for valid lawyerly reasons. But there is no real methodological puzzle here; good Dowkinians have to follow integrity where it leads [...] The trend of deference is not derived from any one judicial decision; it is a global feature of law in the administrate state, observable in many legal systems over time...Law has decided that it best serves its own ends by lying more or less quietly under the throne (2016, pp. 18-22).

It is important to note, however, that the triumph of the administrative state is a second degree Leviathan that rules in the wake of the dismantling of the popular sovereign state. It is as if the state had to compensate the crisis of democratic deliberation with a form of administrative machination. In the void of sovereignty, a new legitimacy is supplemented with an effective form of order that widens its reach, controls, and maintains collective life.

Let us now consider the second case, which should make this problem even more visible. In 2008, the non-profit group Citizens United, who has strong ties to the Tea Party Movement, released a documentary entitled *Hillary: The Movie* (2008), just a few days before the Democratic Primaries. The documentary is replete with apocalyptic overtones, conspiracy tropes, and ultra-nationalist rhetoric as to persuade the spectators that a Hillary Clinton presidency would bring about the Armageddon. The documentary did not see its worldwide screen as scheduled, due to FEC regulations, which led the Citizens United Group to file a demand on the grounds of an unconstitutional violation of the First Amendment. The question that the Roberts Court had to decide was uniquely framed: do corporations have 1st Amendment rights? If so, can we treat them like "persons" and allow them unlimited funding as a condition of speech? In a highly contested opinion, which divided the court 5-4, Justice Kennedy decided in favor of C.U. in these terms:

> By definition, an independent expenditure is political speech presented to the electorate that is not coordinate with a candidate. The fact that a corporation or any other speaks is willing to spend money to try to persuade voters presuppose that they have the ultimate influence over the elected officials. This is inconsistent with many suggestions that the electorate will refuse to take part in a democratic governance because of additional political speech made by a corporation or any other speak (Post, 2014, p. 63).

The opinion decided that corporations can not only influence elections, a precedent that was already in place in *Buckley vs. Valeo* (1976), but more effectively that there was no ceiling to campaign expenditures, since corporations' medium of public speech is money. It follows from this, of course, to the extent that moiney is a medium that amplifies speech, democracy would benefit from the incremental influence of currency in the public. Regulations of financial capital would discourage democratic exchange. Robert Post made clear in his reading of Kennedy's opinion that the decision was oblivious to the fact that the case should not be tailored only around a collective right to speech, but also around the integrity of electoral campaigns. Corporations have rights of speech under the First Amendment, but speech presupposes that we freely speak and remain silent. Money, on the other hand, makes corporations obliged to speak narrowly as "public speech".

Of course, legitimacy in a democratic republic rests upon the belief that political representation is responsive to social needs and concerns. When this fails, legitimacy enters into a crisis, making democracy a mere veneer of administration. If Citizens United means anything it is that, analogous to the administrative state, money becomes the active equivalent for democratic decision and deliberation. Even beyond the relation between money and elections, this decision contributes to erode political parties' structures and to blur the party insiders and those in the shadows such as corporations who favor specific legislation and active political mobilization on the ground (Gerken, 2014, pp. 128-132). The domination of the principle of equivalence turns politics into a mere computational tool for the administration of the whole of social life.

In fact, the effect of the Citizens United's decision brings to effective end political parties as legitimate actors, as new structures in the shadows, corporations, and groups ensamble an opaque anti-democratic fabric. The consummation of the principle of general equivalence as the absolute form of social relations unveils the ruinous foundations of political primacy. In both cases, the administrative state and corporate speech, the People become a sovereign phantom in what is clearly a new epochal transformation.

2. Absolute political legalism

When this occurs, politics and law conflate into a form of policing. In fact, one of the consequences of the fall of legitimacy is a crisis of legality, raising the question as to who belongs in the polis. A figure such as Kris Kobach, current Secretary of the State of Kansas, sheds light on this problem. To just draw a minimal profile of this figure: before graduating from Yale Law School, under the direction of neo-conservative Harvard political scientist Samuel Huntington, Kobach finished his dissertation on the role of political participations of corporations during the apartheid in South Africa, and later in Oxford he completed a book about referendums in Switzerland (1990, 1993). His research is comprehensive, combining his interests on populist plebiscitary mechanisms, and corporate economic designs. In the United States, however, he is known for having drafted the Arizona Bill 1070, which required state police to make irregular arrests of undocumented immigrants wherever there was "reasonable suspension" (Anderson and Smith, 2015). Kobach appears in the context of the constitutional crisis as a representative of a militant politics through internal legalism. As liberal politics transforms into machination and countability, the logic of security emerges as the regulatory moral principle that organizes the space of citizenship. This is very clear if one attentively reads a series of academic articles that Kobach published in 2008, all of them treat the problem of illegal immigration to radically transform our notion of the "citizen".

In "Reinforcing the Rule: What States can Do to Stop Illegal Immigration" Kobach (2008) begins with the economicist premise that a contemporary state cannot be a welfare state and have free migration at the same time. He immediately lays out a detailed set of provisions recommending how states and local authorities could tighten migratory restrictions in order to exert what he calls in another article "attrition through enforcement (2008b): removing social protections, driver's licenses, and higher state education grants to illegal residents. In 2008, Kobach writes a series of articles that, situating himself in the wake of the 9/11 attacks, considers illegal migrants and refugees as always already potential terrorists. Kobach's implicit response to the crisis of democratic legitimacy hinges on three forms of reactionary legal-political tactics: first, a fiscal premise, in which an immigrant is not considered a subject for the expansion of citizenship, but as a burden to taxpayers. Hence, the only possible solution is self-deportation as a more "efficient" economic solution than amnesty.

Secondly, he draws on a legal argument that asks the Federal State to become activist at local and state levels. This is a novel political transformation in United States, since until the 1960s; Republicans and conservative ideologues favored states' rights in order to 'resist' the national government anti-segregation laws passed in the 1950s by the Warren Court. Kobach today emerges as a conservative Hamiltonian who incites states to subordinate their federal sovereignty to the national government. Indeed, Kobach is implicitly situating himself in light of the administrative state in order to break away from what he sees as bureaucratic neutralization. In fact, the dismissal of amnesty is also confrontational to bureaucratic equilibriums in their decision-making. Thirdly, and perhaps more importantly, Kobach perceives citizenship as an assault on a fictive national identity, which is informed after Huntington's last book *Who Are We?: The Challenges to America's National Identity* (2004). In the present, Kobach heads Trump's executive order to establish a Voter Freud Commission, which limits minorities voting access rights and imposes severe registration restrictions for specific electoral filtering. In the wake of *Shelby County vs. Holder*, which limited Article V of the Civil Rights Act of 1965, Kobach emerges as an archaic regression of citizenship rights. This new hegemonic politics instrumentalizes the logic of inclusion-exclusion to construct a politics of belonging. As the "People" disappear as a unifying political principle, the hegemonic phantasm of identity and police take the scene.

3. Not-all democracy

How do we move from the exhaustion of popular sovereignty premised on the citizen in the wake of the administrative state and a legalist political war waged against political life? To tackle to this question, allow me to quote here Bruce Ackerman who asks a similar question in the last chapter "Betrayal"? of his *We The People: Civil Rights Revolution* (2013), where he laments the Roberts Court's decision to overturn Article V of the Civil Rights Acts that protects minority voting rights:

If we hope to sustain the tradition of popular sovereignty into a new century, we cannot afford to cast these leaders as tired epigones living off the constitutional heritage left by the giants of an ever-receding past. We should be reflecting on their achievements – both in adopting New Deal modals to speak for the People and in moving beyond the Frist Reconstruction to establish new egalitarian principles for the modern age (2013, p. 316).

Following this, Ackerman notes, surprisingly, that any possibility for a return of an activist Supreme Court is exhausted, and there is no hope in the horizon that courts will be at the center again. As we have seen before, Kobach's constitutionalism is already what we have described as absolute activist political legalism. An epoch defined by clearly hegemonic contentions for social rights is no longer possible. In light of this predicament, any militant legalism could only amount to a reactive and deficient democratic strategy. The administrative state has displaced courts' hegemony to play a role in taking up the task of enacting a "living constitution". On the other hand, the transformation of the legal tradition is now dominated by capitalist discourse that makes corporations persons, while citizens lose their legal status to become bare life. If constitutionalism can no longer provide for a ground of legitimacy, how can democracy be thought as a region that can no longer coincide with the capitalist discourse?

For legal scholars such as Bruce Ackerman and Dieter Grimm, constitutionalism as a form of legitimation has been on the rise at least since the end of the Second World War. Constitutionalism during the Cold War epoch performed a katechon for democratic building against the perceived communist threat. The fact that constitutions were taken to be models of legitimacy was the novelty, since, modern constitutionalism never figured in typologies of political legitimation. Max Weber for instance, favored charismatic leadership in the figure of the President as equilibrium between political factions and Congress. However, the Weberian charismatic figure today, as Elena Kagan (2001) has demonstrated, is residual as it functions solely on behalf of its administrative authority.

If administrative constitutionalism coincides with the structure of the principle of general equivalence, it means that the task of political thought today is still to break against the dual articulation of this hegemonic closure. In his book *En la frontera: sujeto y capitalismo* (2014), psychoanalyst and political thinker Jorge Alemán, argues that democracy today must be thought in preparation for an «a-theological reparation, a *democracy of desire* – to be precise, the desire to long last together – as we build an alliance with a symbolic order that is beyond the circular movement of capitalist discourse» (2014, p. 109). I want to call this democratic desire against all forms of subjective equivalence (in legal, economic, and political regimes), a posthegemonic democracy that no longer anticipates the absolute and total logic of the social. However, Alemán connects political desire later on in his book to a "freno de mano", a sort of restrainer to the ecstatic movement of financial capital. This metaphor strangely echoes the figure of the katechon, which today can no longer dispense legitimate grounds for politics. We can go further.

Hegemony is a phantasmatic logic that aims for an absolute closure of the social. Posthegemonic democracy, in contrast, is a wake-up call to the insufficiencies of subjective substitutions that promise a total "liberation from history". While political strategies today remain joyfully full of different articulations of the hegemonic phantasm, transformative democratic thought would not seek liberation of the telos of history, but liberation of its fundamental fantasy as the burden that neutralizes politics either towards conflict-resolution (pacification) or to perpetual strife (civil war). These two poles make up the technical-humanism essence of our epoch. This is why choosing one over the other never amounts to a dislocation of its center.

In this light, recent efforts to inscribe federalism, understood as local power and municipal counter-resistance through autonomous politics and practical mobilization, are also limited. Can federal or local mutual aid generate grand politics, or would it remain, necessarily so, a counter-hegemonic alternative oblivious to the ruin of political hegemony in the face of economic and statist structures? (see Gerken, 2009, pp. 14-20). If, according to the great contemporary theorist of progressive federalism Heather Gerken, the sole endgame of federalism today is to displace norms from one side to another, then federal politics is really a tool for reactive politics. Such strategy brings to mind Lenin's theory of the bent stick without amending a new social contract beyond the options already in place. If understood in this way, federalism becomes a sort of "catch-me-if-you-can" game, or as Jon Beasley-Murray called it rather whimsically, a return to "socialism in one state" with different garments. Federalism, as well as communitarian and participatory models of citizen inclusion, becomes an absolutization of locality that covers the void of democratic politics and reducing life to the political. The void within every social contract becomes effaced.

We need to reimagine what democracy means for us today in light of what Alemán calls a "desire to last," which opens to the question of a finite institutionalization as a fissure in the grammar of hegemonic politics. No thinking, and by the same token no "political thought", can take up the task to precede what reality awaits in an epoch that has witnessed the effective decay of interstate sovereign nation states. But if our singular desire is to last, this entails that we need to advance not a fundamental critical theory, but rather a transformative thought that will free the relation of singularity with the social contract in ways that accounts for the impossible desire of the "not-all".

According to philosopher Joan Copjec, the notion of "not-all" of feminine sexuality in Lacan disrupts the logic of extraction and measurement embedded within the grammar of citizenship, as well as every disposition of the subject as that of the "subject that knows". We have repeatedly seen in recent years politics articulated through variations of this formulation: the "People always know", "We the People again", or "it is He Who Speaks for Us." (Copjec, 2002, pp. 12-16). The subject that knows or that "is supposed to know", functions to foreclose the turbulence of history by dissolving it into an efficient mediation between universals and particulars. But the "not-all", as Lacan articulated, exceeds both contradiction and negation, and is irreducible to the valorization of equivalence quipped to administer and unify the hysteric administration of a "politics of the whole".

What I am calling a "not-all" of democracy is neither a politics of partition nor a micropolitics. The excess of the "not-all" remains unthought in every ground of hegemony and outside its vertical cathexis that organizes the unity and guidance of every experience of collective life. To speak of the "not-all" of feminine language against the rhetorical universe of the masculine logic allows for a radically different conceptualization of equality through which the singular's desire escapes the binding economy between politics and life. In other words, the "not-all" of posthegemonic democracy names, if anything, the latency and delirium of an impossible praxis that unworks any attempt to regulate the common goods of one's existence.

References

Ackerman B. (2010). *The Decline and Fall of the American Republic*. Cambridge, MA: Harvard University Press.
Ackerman B. (2013). *We The People: The Civil Rights Revolution*. Vol. 3. Cambridge, MA: Harvard University Press.
Alemán, J. (2014). *En la frontera: sujeto y capitalismo*. Barcelona: Gedisa Editorial.
Anderson K. and Smith M.A. (2015). Appendix: Kris Kobach, the Man behind the Laws. *State Voting laws in America: Historical Statutes and Their Modern Implications*. New York: Palgrave Macmillan.
Arato A. (2016). *Post Sovereign Constitutional Making: Learning and Legitimacy*. Oxford: Oxford University Press.
Copjec J. (2002). *Imagine There's No Woman: Ethics and Sublimation*. Cambridge, MA: MIT Press.
Carrillo S. (1977). *Eurocomunismo y Estado*. Barcelona. Critica (Grijalbo).
Ernst D. (2016). *Tocqueville's Nightmare: The Administrative State Emerges in America, 1900-1940*. Oxford: Oxford University Press.
Gerken H. (2009). Uncooperative Federalism. *Yale Law Journal*, 118/1256.
Gerken H. (2014). The Real Problem with Citizens United: Campaign Finance, Dark Money, and Shadow Parties. *Marquette University Law Review*, 97/4, Summer.
Grimm D. (2017). *The Constitution of European Democracy*. Oxford: Oxford University Press.
Hamburger Ph. (2014). *Is Administrate Law Unlawful?*. Chicago: University of Chicago Press.
Huntington S.P. (2004). *Who Are We?. The Challenges to America's National Identity*. London: Simon & Schuster.
Kagan E. (2001). Presidential Administration. *Harvard Law Review*, 8/114: 2246-2387.
Kobach K.W. (1990). *Political Capital: the Motives, Tactics, and Goals of Politicized Businesses in South Africa*.
Kobach K.W. (1993). *The Referendum: Direct Democracy in Switzerland*.
Kobach K.W. (2008a). Reinforcing the Rule of Law: What

States Can and Should Do to Reduce Illegal Immigration. *Geo Immigration L.J*, 22: 459-483.

Kobach K.W. (2008b). Attrition through Enforcement: a Rational Approach to Illegal Immigration. *Tulsa J. Comp*, 15/2: 155-163.

Kobach K.W. (2008c). *Review*, 36/4: http://www.nationalreview.com/article/213590/liberalsnlawsuits-joseph-6

Lacan J. (1971). *Seminar XVIII: On a Discourse that Might not Be Semblance*. http://www.lacanianworks.net/?p=237

Mashaw J.L. (2012). *Creating the Administrative Constitution: The Lost One Hundred Years of American Administrative Law*. New Haven-London: Yale University Press.

Moreiras A. (2015). Poshegemonía, o más allá del principio del placer. *Poshegemonía: el final de un paradigma de la filosofía política en América Latina*. Madrid: Biblioteca Nueva: 125-140.

Moss D.A. (2017). *Democracy: A Case Study*. Cambridge, MA: Harvard University Press.

Muñoz G. (2017). La Izquierda carece de agenda politica para el siglo XXI: entrevista con Bruce Ackerman". *CTXT*, February. http://ctxt.es/es/20170215/Politica/11142/Entrevista-Bruce-Ackerman-constitucion-Estados-Unidos-Trump.htm.

Muñoz G. (2018). Quietly Laying under the Throne: Essay Review of Adrian Vermeule's *Law's Abnegation: from Law's Empire to the Administrative State*. *Hiedra Magazine*, 9, July.

Posner E. and Vermeule A. (2010). *The Executive Unbound: After the Madisonian Republic*. New York: Oxford University Press.

Post R. (2014). *Citizens Divided: Campaign Finance Reform and the Constitution*. Cambridge, MA: Harvard University Press.

Schlesinger A.M. (1974). *The Imperial Presidency*. Boston-New York: Houghton Mifflin Co.

Sitaraman G. (2017). *The Crisis of the Middle-Class Constitution: Why Economic Inequality Threatens Our Republic*. New York: A.A. Knopf.

Schmitt C. (1927). *Volksentscheid und Volksbegehren. Plebiscite and Referendum*. Berlin: Duncker & Humblot.

Schmitt C. (1987). The Legal World Revolution. *Telos*: 73-89.

Vermeule A. (2016). *Law's Abnegation: from Law's Empire to the Administrative State*. Cambridge, MA: Harvard University Press.

Enrica Lisciani-Petrini
NOTES ON THE PARADIGM OF "SUBJECT"

1. *Premise*

Why should we return to the problem of the "subject"? Is it not the framework on which the entire philosophic thought of the 20th century focused with a view to deconstructing it? This is certainly true. However, let's set ourselves some questions: can we say that that deconstruction has had a satisfactory outcome, that new frameworks and forms of "subjectivation" have been identified, to put it as Foucault would? It would not seem so. On the other hand, and at the very least: has it not been noted that the old subject paradigm is now unusable? Or, at the very least, has some confusion not been registered regarding the latter? No. To the contrary, the notion of subject is still considered obvious and taken for granted by many. They even consider it uncontrollable and such that it does not contain any kind of "ambiguity" and therefore does not justify any kind of surrounding interrogation.

Thus today we find ourselves before a paradoxical situation, which is both double-faced and contradictory. On the one hand – with the development of deconstruction and of globalisation – it was thought that taking away every limit from the subject would disseminate it into an infinite web of porous and indistinct differences: into a multitude of many "others", within which every self-referential identity would be dissolved and surpassed. On the other hand – and from an eminently re-active view with regard to the first process – identitarian and auto-referential closures, walls and fenced off profiles, were erected to protect the "sovereign" subject or the "sovereign" identity of, say, a country, a nation, or a single state that feels menaced by that dissolutionary thrust. And it is along this last axis that the paradigm of the "subject" comes back to impose itself, like a unique safeguard and, together with this, as something that is absolutely obvious, like I was saying earlier, in its rootedness and usefulness. As is readily comprehensible, this process – which is both identitarian and reactive and still subjectivist – is nothing but the other side of the latter – that is, dissolutionary, globalising, anti-subjectivist. Consequently one supports the other, almost as though the two sides were inseparable like those of a Janus face. This determines an aporetic situation of deadlock, or a potentially explosive and conflicting one, where the old hatreds and phobias re-emerge. However, "old" and "ancient" are just expressions, because they are in fact always alive under the surface and ready to burst out into the open.

That is why it is necessary to go back to the paradigm of the subject, to get off the path leading to this double and contradictory entanglement; and to try to understand how it is possible to identify a new form of "subjectivation" to match globalisation and its intrinsic problems. A new historical and political entity, which would lie beyond the dissolution of every limit and so be able to, on the one hand, re-propose a determined political "subject", but, on the other hand, to avoid re-proposing unequivocally

identitarian closures. To this end, it is necessary to conduct, first and foremost, a historical and genealogical analysis, to take another comprehensive look at how and when the "subject" paradigm was born within modernity. And, going even deeper, it is also necessary to assess, in line with Heidegger, from which idea of being in general is born the notion of the modern "subject": that is, from which "essential decision". For the implications of this decision, in many respects, have lasted up until today.

2. *A brief excursus on the birth of the framework of the subject*

Naturally, here, in the little space that I have at my disposal, I must limit myself to sketching out the rough outlines of the long semantic and cultural path spanning multiple centuries that produced the constitution of the "modern subject". But these will suffice to provide us with the indications that we need – which are indispensable – for our future considerations.

2.1

As is well known, the "subjectum" – in the sense that is still used today – was born in the 17th century. Not with Descartes – as is commonly thought because of a reconstruction and interpretation that was literally invented by Kant, then summarised by Hegel and continued by Husserl and Heidegger. To the contrary, it began with Locke, with the completion of a series of complex passages and developments that went on from Roman times, along to medieval times until finally reaching the modern era. Before modernity – and this should be highlighted – *subjectum* had an entirely different meaning: it referred to the foundation, the substrate (the *hypokeimenon*) of something (or in the sense of the *sub-stantia*, of the "substance" of the real; or in the sense in which, for example, today we say "the subject of that discourse is ...").

How, then, did the passage from *"sub-jectum"* (hypokeimenon) as a "substrate" underlying the modern "subject agent" (*subjectum*) occur? Above all, it was through a process of chiastic interpolation and contamination, through which, already in the Scholastic era, three principles were brought together and made to interact: "the [logico-grammatical] principle of the denomination of the subject [*hypokeimenon*] through the accident", the "[ontological] principle of subjectivation of the action to the power of an agent", with the other principle according to which "actiones sunt suppositorum" (= the actions are un/attributed to "suppositions", that is, every action must have its own foundation, its own *hypostasis*). The "subject" thereby becomes the foundation – the *hypostasis,* the substrate – of its own actions. This first comprehensive operation of logical and ontological restructuring of the "subject" (which, from being the substrate of reality has now become the nominal and factual substrate of an accidental action) is a basis for future developments (see de Libera, 2007-8, I, pp. 50-51 and ss).

In fact it is especially through the successive operations conducted by Locke that the "subject" became an "individual and personal substance" "conscious of itself". To reach this ulterior (and definitive) transformation Locke brings two elements into play. Firstly the notion of "person" – which, as is known, makes its entry into philosophy through Boerzio. The term *person* in the patristic age was employed as a synonym of *hypostasis*, that is to say, with a meaning (as we saw a little earlier) that explicitly referred to the notion of substrate, of foundation. This is how the category of *person* can interlink with the principle that I highlighted earlier – the underlying subject as a substrate, a foundation of its own actions – and thereby embed itself within the nascent category of "subject". And since the person, as Boezio asserts, is an "individual substance", in this manner the notion of person confers that "unity" on the "subject agent" that makes it the unique and *individual* focal point around around which all its acts revolve.

But that is not all. Locke completes an additional probe into scholasticism. He summarises the ancient notion of *kategoría*, both in the sense, precisely, of "attribution" to the subject of the action – for which it becomes a proper "subject agent"; and in the other sense of the term: "accusation" or "imputation". And so, it is precisely this last meaning that allows Locke to identify in the "subject agent" its effort to impute acts to itself, which presuppose "consciousness" in so far as the latter «reminds the "self" its accomplished thoughts and acts» so that, as Locke writes in his *Essay on human intellect,* «personality extends beyond present existence up until the past, and with this it becomes implicated in the latter and *becomes responsible for it*» (Locke, 1971, II, XXVII, § 28, p. 407, *my italics*) – and therefore imputable.

The process is thereby completed. From this secular trend that ties together multiple conceptual threads – the "substrate", which has multiple and ancient meanings, with the person, now understood as a consciousness that imputes elements to itself – is born the modern "personal agent subject". This is the mainstay of any subjectivism. The subject is centred on its own autonomous and rational consciousness and closed in by its own insurmountable individuality.

2.2

But let's take a closer look. On further inspection – and on the basis of this admittedly brief genealogical reconstruction – the "personal agent subject" appears to constitute itself within its completed profile *just because a schism is produced in the latter*. This is a hierarchical separation between a part of itself, the "spiritual" and rational dimension, that instead slides toward the other and watches, "imputing" to itself, the self's accomplished acts, from a, by definition, paramount, or sovereign, position; and another side of itself (the corporeal-material dimension), that instead slides downwards becoming, by definition, an inferior part, dominated and so literally "subjected" to the former. This split thereby produces, from now on, the calcification of a framework that fixes the image of man within a double and ineffable range. On the one hand, man is an entity unambiguously endowed with a rational spirit and so in a state of constitutive transcendence. On the other hand, he indeed has a substrate that is both physical and biological, but this, by virtue of the "governing" of reason, of the "freedom of sovereign will", can be "governed", i.e. shaped so as to subjugate the original instinctual and corporeal layer and make it become the external manifestation of the interior presence of reason (as is often said: from the expression and posture of a person emerges his/her "spirit", his/her "internal soul", that shapes the persons' movements and characteristics). This is peculiar to the division of man into two parts – where the second (corporeal) part is subsumed only in so far as it is *subjugated* by the other (rational) part – and is therefore at the basis of the constitution of the "modern subject" as a "person".

The process of personalisation, therefore, advances alongside the radical oustering from the "person subject" of everything that is impersonal (that which does not belong to the personal individual and cannot be attributed to its rationality) and, together with this and to the contrary, with the strengthening of all those "properties" – in the double sense of "characteristics" (physical and/or moral) and "interests or material goods" – that compete to manufacture a supremely individualised and unrepeatable "self", enclosed within the perimeter of its own unique "proprietary" identity.

2.3

But from where does this division originate? From which vision of the whole of reality, that is, from which "essential decision", to use Heidegger's words, would, does such a constitution of the "agent subject" originate? Well, from a vertical perspective, going to the root of what is produced within modernity, we realise that – firstly and most radically – it is the world itself that is «split as it were into two worlds», as Husserl incisively proclaimed (1983, p. 89): into a heavy rational dimension and into another extended and calculable material one. According to the decisive Cartesian programme, where the second appears to be completely subjugated by the first, which, from this moment onward, will make it a "place" at the "disposal" of its own "disposition" (see Heidegger, 1973). And it is this first preliminary and original division, at the ontological level, that presides over the, let's say, anthropological split of man himself who is, on the one hand, rational and, on the other hand, corporeal, extended and inferior. But this is not all. Precisely the fact that the material dimension has been reduced – i.e. concrete, corporeal and living reality – to a "calculable" extension is what rapidly reduces the latter to a mere quantity that is subjected to measurement. And it is, once again, from here that the reduction of his/her own person into a calculable person is produced within man himself, so much so that his/her individuality is all the more distinguished the more quantifiably measurable characteristics it possesses. In this manner, men are reduced not only to mere "factual men", to use the Husserlian terminology, but moreover and especially to mere measurable entities. This means that they are measurable in terms of their homogeneous quantities and not their heterogeneous qualities, as Bergson picked up on with great sagacity, at what is by now the other end of modernity (see Bergson, 1995).

3. Towards a unique "subject"

Until here, then, we have reconstructed, in line with what we had set ourselves, the genealogy of the "modern subject" and the posterior ontological structure (decision) that supports it. Now we are able to see the origin of anthropology, as well as the ethics and politics that came later. These are still relevant to our times and we monitor them constantly – even when we are not aware of it and do not pay attention to it.

In fact – just to indicate some eminent aspects – it is completely evident that in a society that is founded on this "system", or *Gestell* as Heidegger would call it, or rather on this framework of categories, we are only representative and "individualised" to the extent that we are the "owners" to various degrees of "goods" and of "properties". However, this excludes all those people who do not possess any of these elements (for instance, migrants that arrive on our lands with nothing). And it is precisely this individualism, bearing a modern character, that is at the origin of economic and political liberalism and, together with this, of that myth of the individual, of the person and of property (or of the wealth and capital) that began to characterise global politics and economics since the 17th century – and which slowly but surely reached our era, with all the perversions that derive from the latter. For example, with the uninhibited use of the market, which in our time is the cause of iniquitous and increasing inequalities at the global level, accompanied by, to this day, an increasing, and ever more extreme, financialization that reduces men and their lives to mere numerical and quantitative functions/expressions; and following this – just as Simone Weil clearly saw in her time – with that uncontrollable self-promoting individualism, which often overpowers others (Weil, 2012), and which now seems to have become a prevalent anthropomorphic and psychological characteristic, especially among the young. For the latter, the recent numerical, quantitative and not qualitative, valuation (the mercantile and economic language symptomatic of the issue) of the "products" of research and intellectual creativity is not at all foreign. This is what results in all this "identitarian" political side-taking that is re-emerging in growing measure. It is where we started and toward and where we are coming back with a renewed individualistic closure: new nationalisms, new regionalisms, new isolationisms, "small nations" and so forth. These are all the heightened effects of that "autonomously agentive and individual subject" which originated in the 17th century.

Of course, as I was saying earlier, these consequences, and particularly on a political level, are also the fruit of intercultural and transnational globalisation, the very same that produced the rupture of all identitarian and subjective bounds. Globalisation indeed seemed of a nature that could be enthusiastically welcomed and favoured, in so far as it was able to produce – against an individualistic liberalism that was closed in on itself – an extra-subjective and ultra-identitarian «multitude, and so to bring us to an ultra-nationalist and statist government of the world» (Negri and Hardt, 2004). In reality, however, globalisation was not only able to realise this expansive and "unifying" political process, but to the contrary – as we now know retrospectively – it has produced two perverse counter effects. On the one hand, precisely, it has determined and is determining the reactive and defensive re-emergence of immunitary political mechanisms and processes (see Esposito, 2000). On the other hand, it has determined a counter effect that can even be said to be paradoxical, because capitalistic and economic liberalism has exploited this very transnational borderlessness in order to strengthen its own capitalist machine at a global level. This has contributed, in turn, to incrementing those same defensive mechanisms of "re-enclosure" within indentitary and national borders.

In short, the categorical framework that originates from this tradition, by now, foreshadows so many aporias and contradictions that it makes urgent the task of overcoming both the individualistic and liberal subject, on one side, and its antithesis, on the other, that is, the ultra-subjectivasation or the dissolution of subjectivism, advanced within the thought of dissemination and of globalisation. In view of a new form of cultural and therefore political entity, that escapes both the individualistic framework and the modern subject, and the unlimited dissemination of the globalised and simply intercultural subject. It is therefore necessary to reach what one could call the "interpersonal subject". Naturally, what I am now about to say does not at all pretend to give answers to the many questions arising from our times and nor to propose a solution. For one, because I do not have the political competencies but also because philosophy can only raise issues and at most offer ways through which to engage upon reflection. Consequently, and with this precise knowledge, I conclude by briefly outlining what I mean by "impersonal subject".

For one, the "impersonal subject" is a notion that has a lot to do with what two specific philosophers were saying: especially Merleau-Ponty and, in some ways, Deleuze – when they spoke of the "institution" (*Stiftung*): i.e. how within history a "form" gets instituted that is determined but not closed. That is how a political "subject" is formed. But in order to grasp this point it is necessary to return to an ontological perspective, to a vision that is in the background of Merleau-Ponty's and Deleuze's work. Without attempting to produce a complete outline, we can say that today – compared to the traditional ontological terrain recalled earlier, that divides reality on two distinct levels: a transcendental upper level and lower immanent and subjugated one – we are by now in a situation that sees transcendence as rooted in immanence, in a pre-categorical (even instinctual) substrate that precedes man's posited activity. This means seeing every determined form *not* as the result of an "abstract" decision (treated outside) of concrete reality, but as separated from the latter and lowered down from above, from a sovereign position, and consequently inscribed within a framework prevalently characterised by a intellectualistic logic that is closed in on itself (as it was for the modern subject) – *but* only as the product of the concrete and mobile interrelations embedded within historical and material reality. The "institution" – as Merleau-Ponty and early Deleuze say – originates from the very terrain of life. This is the same as what occurs in the biological dimension, where forms that are adapted to the *entire* surrounding environment are continually produced.

But what does this bring to the historical and political field? It shows that every form that emerges, every "subject" that is produced, cannot be the fruit of an abstract decision willed by someone's mind on the basis of an unequivocal and closed profile. To the contrary, it is the result of a mobile process that happens through time. Moreover, its relations *enter to constitute that given form, that given subject.* Therefore the "subject" that is produced in this way cannot be the effect of the closing in on itself of a given identity, of a single "person", that is conceived on the basis of a rational pre-given framework, but it is a combination of relations that, yes, gives itself limits, but at the same time encompasses those multiple relations from which it emerges and to which it remains tethered. Consequently a subject that is conceived in this way is intrinsically – not casually or only at certain times, but always and constitutively – impersonal or, considers itself "interpersonal". And in addition it is conceived as the person *and* the impersonal – just like the two inseparable sides of the same coin. It is that subject and, *together* with this, the whole combination of the connections that constitute it. This is precisely because an insular and individual subject does not exist in any shape or form – it is merely a modern invention.

Consequently an institution, a political subject, is produced thanks to a chiasmus between determination (containment perimeter) and pluri-relationality. These are two aspects that should be thought of *together* and are *born together.* Because pluri-relationality does not live without limits, without determinations that contain it (the same way an organism does not live without a body that contains it); and the determination, the border, is only formed through *that* pluri-relationality, for *that* organism. Not therefore, again, as something that comes from above and is rationalistically, intellectually determined, but something that is born *from* the very historical context, from the *milieu*, as Merleau-Ponty would say, echoing (as Deleuze does as well) the *Umwelt* of Uexküll (2015).

On exiting all this discourse, which could seem merely theoretical, one could ask: what does this mean concretely? What does it mean, for instance, that Europe cannot be an entity or an abstractly configured identity based upon merely economic and financial parameters or intellectual ones? The fact is that it can neither be a sort of historical and cultural magma destined to be dissolved and lose its own identity. And nor can it be the vacuum containing many small identities that want – again abstractly, outside of the concrete processes of present history – to be sovereign or, as we say today, "pro-sovereignty" with regard to their own state and national configuration. It is just as though, today, we did not realise that the state, the nation, are dead and exhausted paradigms. Therefore, the "impersonal and political subject" – for instance, Europe today – is the one that maintains the need for a border, for the determination of the classic "subject", but, in contrast to this, it does *not* restrict itself to a unique identity – to a unique "person" we could say, to a sole nation, that is to be safeguarded. *Instead* it understands within itself the multiple plural-identities for which, today, the historical contexts, like Europe, are now formed. For this "impersonal and political subject", having a pluri-identity therefore means that, in addition to its own identitarian character, which one could call national or "personal", it has *contemporaneously* ultra-identitarian characters, or impersonal ones – because they are intrinsically correlated to all the other political identities to which they are tied within a single historical complex. Thus it is only by starting from the grassroots of effective, historical life, and of the effective and concrete inter-relation I have discussed, and only *from here*, that a new political entity should emerge. Precisely: an "impersonal subject".

References

Balibar E., ed. (1998). *John Locke. Identité et différence. L'invention de la conscience* (French translation of *Essai philosophique concernant l'entendement humain* by Locke). Paris: Seuil.
Balibar E. (2011). *Citoyen sujet et autres essais d'anthropologie philosophique*. Paris: PUF.
Balibar E., Cassin B. et de Libera A. (2004). Sujet: Subjectivité et assujettissement. In B. Cassin (ed.), *Vocabulaire européen des philosophies*. Paris: Seuil.
Bergson H. (1932). *Les deux sources de la morale et de la religion*. Paris: Alcan. Trad. it. *Le due fonti della morale e della religione*. Milano, Cortina 2002.
de Libera A. (2007-2008). *Archéologie du sujet* (I: *Naissance du sujet*; II; *La quête de l'identité*). Paris: Vrin.
Deleuze G., ed. (1955). *Istinti e istituzioni*, a cura di U. Fadini e K. Rossi. Milano: Mimesis 2014.
Esposito R. (2000). *Immunitas. Protezione e negazione della vita*. Torino: Einaudi.
Esposito R. (2013). *Due. La macchina della teologia politica e il posto del pensiero*. Torino: Einaudi.
Husserl E. (1983). *La crisi delle scienze europee e la fenomenologia trascendentale*. Firenze: Il Saggiatore.
Heidegger M. (1973). L'epoca dell'immagine del mondo. In: *Sentieri interrotti*. Firenze: La Nuova Italia.
Lisciani-Petrini E. (2007). Fuori della persona. L'"impersonale" in Merleau-Ponty, Bergson, Deleuze. *Filosofia politica*, 3.
Lisciani-Petrini E. (2012). Verso il soggetto impersonale. *Filosofia Politica*, 1.

Lisciani-Petrini E. (2014). La fine della vita eroica. *Filosofia Politica*, 1.
Locke J. (1971). *Saggio sull'intelletto umano*. Torino: UTET.
Marramao G. (2010), *Passaggio a Occidente. Filosofia e globalizzazione*. Torino: Bollati Boringhieri (english: *The Passage West*, Verso, London-New York 2012.
Marramao G. (2013). *Dopo il Leviatano. Individuo e comunità*. Torino: Bollati Boringhieri.
Merleau-Ponty M. (1995). *Lingua Storia Natura. Corsi al Collège de France 1952-1960*, a cura di M. Carbone, Milano: Bompiani.
Merleau-Ponty M. (2003). *L'institution. La passivité. Notes de cours au Collège de France 1954-1955*. Paris: Belin.
Negri A. and Hardt M. (2004). *Moltitudine. Guerra e democrazia nel nuovo ordine imperiale*. Milano: Rizzoli.
Resta C. (2016). *La passione dell'impossibile. Saggi su Jacques Derrida*. Genova: il Melangolo.
Uexküll J. von (2015). *Biologia teoretica*, a cura di L. Guidetti. Macerata: Quodlibet.
Weil S. (2012). *La persona e il sacro*. Milano: Adelphi.

Yoandy Cabrera

PODEMOS
Between the Affect and the *Habitus*

In a stroke of his genius, Aeschylus puts into the mouths of the enemies, the Persians, his conceptualization of Athenian democracy. Said conceptualization is closer to the post-hegemonic than to that of the Greeks themselves, contemporaries to tragedy, while proposing a transversality that is still unknown in today's Western political praxis. The 15-M in Spain, in spite of the differences, seems to approach the fictional Aeschylean democracy. «And what king is above them and sends his army?» – asks Queen Atossa to the corypheus. And he replies: «They are not called slaves or subjects of any man» (*The Persians*, v. 243-44). Immediately, one discovers in Aeschylus a tendency to non-subjection as a principle of the democratic. The Queen, from her hegemonic mentality, does not understand how an army without an absolute leader has been able to defeat the mighty Persian army. The radicalization carried out by Aeschylus, from the Athenian practice to the fictional sphere, is what the post-hegemonic demands today to go from the Aeschylean fiction to the political praxis. The 15-M movement in Spain illustrates a possible way of that leap from the tragedy to the reality in the 21st century.

It is necessary to begin, however, at the incident, the timely moment, the opening or *kairós* that the 15-M movement brought to Spanish society and specifically the emergence of Podemos (*We Can*). The incident which the traditional politicians cataloged as unacceptable, illegal, illicit, useless, the gesture of some misfits. Politicians that would later be in charge of flirting with the 15-M to scrape a few votes. A movement that was made possible to what now has been reduced to just one or two paragraphs in the new programs of the different factions of *Podemos* presented in Vista Alegre II. My reaction to the continuous demands of the militants of "unity, unity" during the congress of this young political organization in Vista Alegre II was thinking if they were not forgetting something, something substantial and basic, something that was already said and questioned in a sort of practical way in what happened those days of May of 2011 in Puerta del Sol. The plurality, the divergence, the concept of the "people" as an amorphous system that Agustín García Calvo talks about and that is related to the concept of "crowds" that we read in Deleuze, Bourdieu and Negri was a palpable reality in the Spanish *plazas* at that time. That was a present that disbelieved in any promise of a tomorrow and that seemed to settle in a sustained today. García Calvo himself participated in the encampment at the Puerta del Sol and from there insisted on the dangers that such an spontaneous and plural movement could face if swallowed by more traditional politics. In turn, the Spanish politicians most visible in 2011, and especially those of the party in the government, protested against the mobilizations. These protests were motivated either because they claimed the encampments were not authorized, affected the regular functioning of downtown, or because they were potentially harmful to the hygiene of the capital and were potential sources of infection. In conclusion: because they were supposedly not part of the legal, domesticated and healthy body of Spanish society. And these same politicians in the government from that moment onwards demanded that, if the protesters had something to say, they should put it forward following the laws of what they insisted on calling "democratic game". Podemos comes from the attempt to crystalize those voices through the channels of traditional Spanish politics.

The consolidation of the party behind a strategic leader, a figure visible and recognizable through the cameras and the mass media, an empty signifier that is increasingly less so, is a danger that Podemos faces since coming out into the public arena. Iñigo Errejón, for instance, with his divergent proposal – although he himself submits to the rhetoric in favor of unity that the militants demanded every few minutes during the presentation of the various projects – seems to be suggesting or leaning towards a different model of that carried out by the party. Podemos appeared on the political map of Spain against a decades set establishment.

Little by little, after a more radical discourse at its inception, the organization decided to play by the rules of traditional politics so that once in power, it would change things around. Therefore, Podemos' plan seems to be to play with the cards of hegemony and its concepts so once in power it can try to go a little further.

They have begun to use the language of traditional politics and more familiar to Spanish society (homeland, unity, nation, identity etc.) to supposedly approach their sensitivity; they have adopted as politics a simulation of affection that allows them to come to power. They have wanted to play traditional politics when their goal has always seemed to be to try "something else", play with different and new concepts. In this charade, in this rhetorical replay, there is a concealment that becomes a mask and perpetuates the same hegemonic game that it aims to combat.

Vista Alegre II was "the" missed opportunity (opportunity hopefully only postponed) to make of divergences a different weapon to that of traditional politics. We are used to seeing a party with different views and opinions that overlap once a vote is imposed for the alleged unity of the party. It is what continues to happen until today in the PP and the PSOE. But Podemos, if we go back to the 15-M movement, started being or at least seemed to be "something else".

In May of 2011 I lived in Méndez Álvaro 4, on one of the sides of Puerta de Atocha. I was always walking to Puerta del Sol and crossing through Montera to get to Gran Vía. From these daily journeys comes my short relationship with the 15-M: in the mornings, in the afternoons, at night, I would go by and go to the stalls where they would distribute food, or to the diverse meetings on economy, education and other subjects that were made in different assemblies around the streets near the plaza. Puerta del Sol was a place of unity and brotherhood without being a place where some subjugated others, without a figure being erected as a representation of a phenomenon that was, and still is, indefinable. It was a space of confrontation and dialogue, in which anyone could ask permission to speak and expose certain ideas that were part of the debate, a debate that was not always harmonious and rather tense at times. One could be part of that varied crowd or follow along in their walk without even asking permission. A pluralistic, amorphous body that today might seem utopian, was a reality in the Spanish squares.

In the public letter that Pablo Iglesias writes to Íñigo Errejón on December 12, 2016, affection and *habitus* are apparently confused at the convenience of Iglesias, speaking in infrapolitical terms, to perpetuate the hegemonic. Iglesias says that the reason he writes to Errejón is «to tell you the same thing he would say in one of our chats». The sender matches the space of affection and intimacy with the *res publicae*. Iglesias, in addition, clarifies that «today it is not your secretary general who writes to you, but rather your partner and your friend» (*ibid.*), so that it emphasizes the affective space as point of enunciation. This is not the case analyzed by Beasley-Murray in which affection becomes habit (2010); what Iglesias seems to be doing is, using a rhetoric that is confused with affection in such a way that it becomes a hegemonic action without appearing to be so. His rhetoric, which Giacomo Marramao calls «mirrored» (2020), seems to want to confuse the infrapolitical space with the political one, a gesture that becomes deceptive in that it ends up freezing the friend, the other, his project and ideas. However, what one would expect from Podemos, from the experience of 15-M, would be to tend to what Marramao presents as a necessary politics of the present. That is, to strengthen the relationship through interaction and contradictions, those that Alberto Moreiras (2017) calls "antagonisms", where not only the diverse lines are presented, but interact and live together continuously. As Marramao affirms, the political order does not neutralize the civil war – or at least should not try to neutralize it. Civil war should constitute politics, and I believe that this can be understood not from Podemos outwards, but precisely inwards: civil war, rivalry, contradictions, should always be taken into account as a constituent part of political practice.

Iglesias' gesture freezes alternative projects instead of maintaining interaction with them as part of Podemos' policy. Iglesias, therefore, perpetuates the fundamental problem of hegemony that, according to Jorge Álvarez Yágüez (2019), is not allowing the entrance to pluralities, to be coercive in the face of plurality. Following Yágüez, the totalizing should be, precisely, that which perpetuates the participation of plurality. This way we would be closer to the post-hegemony that, as Beasley-Murray affirms: «proposes a policy of experimentation rather than solidarity, an open policy even to the possibility of betrayal, even of self-treason» (2010, p. 160).

The concept of "multitude", following Beasley-Murray's approach, could be understood as a constant updating of the Aristotelian *me panta*. A policy in which the systematization is not based on making the inapprehensible a closed concept seems necessary. Sometimes the limits of metaphysics seem clearer when trying to match an open meaning (the crowd) with a closed and daringly illusory sign (the people), when we circumscribe the ungraspable to broad hegemonic metaphors as homeland, nationalism, or unity. Podemos could rise up against that politically grammatical metaphysical closure embodied in the concept of people, but the political organization perpetuates the tendency of traditional politics of turning the multitude into a people. Podemos gets lost coming from the crowd, in the desperate task of wanting to build people within hegemonic tradition.

From the 15-M movement to the present of Podemos, there is a crisis in the political architecture of modernity. Taking into account the many differences between Latin America and Europe, there is a danger that threatens enterprises such as the Bolivian project of the last few years and the one of Podemos: the tendency to perpetuate a charismatic leader turned icon that seems increasingly indispensable. The various attempts of the Bolivian government to change the electoral system so that Evo Morales can be re-elected after finishing the allotted years of his mandate seem to point to the failure of a project that promised to tend towards transversality and not to the iconization of a leader. In Podemos the facts point towards a similar situation, even though Iglesias repeats again and again the opposite. This is not only due to the visibility of the general secretary but also to the strategies carried out to govern in cities such as Barcelona and Madrid, using figures that have become, before or after arriving at the government, iconic leaders. Iglesias speaks of a decentralization that contradicts the implementation of a program that leaves at least frozen the other possible alternatives, the other programs presented. The rejection of any form of transcendence in Deleuze should be read in these political projects through the questioning of the existence of an indisputable leader. In the same way that Podemos erects certain formulas of the so-called minorities to legitimize and make themselves visible, it should take into account those projects that have become minority in the core of their party and have them as eligible instead of paralyzing them. It would be good to look towards 1-M as an implementation of what Beasley-Murray calls a politics of the affections and what Peter Baker (2019) calls policies of the crowd, where they inhabit the transversality and contradictions.

Alberto Moreiras would point out to these as the foundations of a possible democratic populism, in which both terms are taken to radicalization to achieve, according to Moreiras, «a democratic populism, anarchic, parrhesia, marrano, and post hegemonic»:

> It is convenient to eliminate the "leader function" – Moreiras says – of the theory of hegemony –against Bonapartism – , in the medium term, we must go towards what others are calling anarcho-populism, or citizenship, that is, populism without leaders.

What Beasley-Murray (2010) proposes, «a politics of affection according to a post hegemonic age» (p. 126), remains a pending task in current political practice. It would, then, seem necessary to return to fiction, to Aeschylus, to the conceptualization that the tragedy achieved better than the political practice. It would be a challenge, therefore, to make democracy coincide with posthegemony, transversality and antagonism; whereas the hegemonic should be increasingly relegated to the oligarchic verticality, to the image of Queen Atossa who, totally paralyzed and surprised, wonders how it could have been.

References

Baker P. (2019). *Politics of the Multitude: Seven Theses on Posthegemony*.

Beasley-Murray J. (2010). *Posthegemonía. Teoría política y América Latina*. Minneapolis-London: University of Minnesota Press.

Iglesias ??.

Marramao G. (2020). *Towards a New Concept of the Political*, in this volume.

Alberto Moreiras A. (2017). Plomo hegemónico en las alas, I. La hipótesis Podemos. Borrador. *Infrapolital Deconstruction*, April 9.

Yágüez J.A. (2020). *Limits of the Concept of Hegemony*. Gramsci and Laclau-Mouffe. In this volume.

SECTION 3

PEOPLE, COMMUNITY, MULTITUDE

Teresa M. Vilarós

THE ELEPHANT AND THE SOVEREIGN ALL OVER AGAIN

> This is how we've ended up, with the elephant's proboscis
> Gramsci, from a letter from prison to his son Delio, 1936

Responding to the hypothetical question posed by his son Delio on whether the elephant would ever be capable of evolving and dominating nature, like man, and be able to use his enormous size, columnar legs, impressive tusk, extra-large flat ears, and huge, flexible proboscis for his own ends, Antonio Gramsci wrote to him from prison that «the elephant has not had the same development as man and certainly will not have it because man uses the elephant, while the elephant cannot use man, not even to eat him» (Gramsci, 1994, p. 381). The boy's query was hypothetical, even playful, while the father's answer, while keeping a festive tone, was very much on the side of the serious, sounding even a bit upset: «there is too much anthropomorphism in your hypotheses» – he snaps – «[w]hy should the elephant have evolved like a man […] You have told me that you liked history and this is how we've ended up, with the elephant's proboscis» (*ibid.*). That Gramsci did not want the elephant to ever evolve like man seems clear. He does not want that most amazing animal to reach any kind of dominance over nature, or over man. None.

And not because maybe Gramsci would favor human hegemony over a hypothetical animal hegemony, but because he, after all a son of the island that John Berger described in a poetic way as primitive and stony, still seems somehow to look at the animals also in a "primitive", non-industrial way.In any case, and while Gramsci's last remark was made in reference to his son's supposed interest in history and was not meant to imply that history itself was ending up like a severed elephant's proboscis, this letter is far from displaying his more usual assertiveness on hegemonic action in the age of chaos. On the contrary, here Gramsci's letter is closer to the kind of infrapolitical writing Michele Cometa detected in some of his prison texts:

> We are aware, of course, that Gramsci's and Benjamin's thought can be considered as a part of the hegemonic and counter-hegemonic way of thinking which is *malgré tout* a continuation of the onto-theology of politics. Nevertheless, if we look at the forms of Gramsci's writing in prison or Benjamin's writing in exile, at the development in their practice of writing, we will see a slow but inexorable development from a traditional way of speaking about politics to a new form that takes the structure of an infrapolitical thinking. Infrapolitics is not only a way to act but also to write (2016, p. ????).

Taking into consideration that the year the letter was written was 1936, we can intuit an infrapolitical register in Gramsci's exchange with his son Delio on the technical abilities of the elephant that extends to his visualization of the history of Europe as a detached elephant's trunk. A register that echoes «the never-ending work of de-metaphorization». Cometa, following Alberto Moreiras's understanding of the infrapolitical, sometimes perceives in Gramsci's prison letters.

The way the exchange over the elephant happens in Gramsci's letter is a de-metaphorizing exercise that, moving away from any plea for hegemonic action, approaches the infrapolitical. Granted that to Delio's playful and imaginative proposals on how cool it would be if the elephant «could have stood upright on his hind legs in order to better develop his brain», or, if he would have had the «ability to adapt his hooves for practical labor», «the father's answers aim to cut back his son's phantasy flights in a non-inventive way. He scolds the son for wasting his time; all those "ifs" do not correspond to reality, he tells him, I believe that to study history one mustn't fantasize too much about what might have happened 'if' […] It is already very difficult to study the history that really did take place […] why would one waste time positing hypotheses that have no foundation?» (Gramsci, 1994, p. 381). And yet, with his comments, and, especially, with his visualization of the elephant's trunk as the image of history circa 1936, Gramsci actually makes a de-metaphorizing opening towards something other than politics and history that includes the elephant – and nature – "as is": alive, and not subjected to exploitation by humans. He refuses to imagine the possibility of animals using humans, he fervently does not want to envision the elephant achieving human technical capabilities; and not because he would support modernity's overwhelming, necro-technological use of animals and nature, but because, on the contrary, in the now of the letter, and from prison, Gramsci, a Sardinian at heart, seems genuinely to prefer that humans would have never stopped looking at animals – and animals at humans – the way they did until the industrial revolution.

And how was that gaze? Berger again, in an essay where he discusses the containment of animals in zoos, notes that before the age of industrialization, before the actual zoo was celebrated as urban entertainment, and animals became thoroughly used up and wasted, «[t]he eyes of an animal when they consider a man [were] attentive and wary» Man in turn, he says, «was aware of himself returning the look»:

> When man is *being seen* by the animal, he is being seen as his surroundings are seen by him. His recognition of this is what makes the look of the animal familiar. And yet the animal is distinct, and can never be confused with man. Thus, a power is ascribed to the animal, comparable with human power but never coinciding with it. The animal has secrets which, unlike the secrets of caves, mountains, seas, are specifically addressed to man. (2009, p. 12).

Any secrets to be perceived have certainly been lost in the age of light and reason, after the onset of industrialization. From then on, a time when for the first time in history the meat of animals started being mass-marketed for consumption, and wild animals became marginalized in urban zoos, that old, pre-industrialization gaze between animal and man Berger tells us about, that look «which may have played a crucial role in the development of human society, and with which, in any case, all men had always lived until less than a century ago, has been extinguished. This historic loss, to which zoos are a monument» – he states somberly – «is now irredeemable for the culture of capitalism» (*ibid.*). The culture of capitalism certainly has lost that look; but, also the animal. In April 2018, a road accident in Spain involving a circus truck carrying elephants, which resulted in the death of one and injuries to others, caught the people's attention and excited their imagination. This is how a Marxist blog described the pouring of sympathy by the people and the media:

> In the accident in question, no one had died. Only an elephant. Four others walked, bruised, along the central reservation of the motorway. The next day the media had already informed us, in detail, about the lives of those beasts in the circus in which they worked. Today there was no newspaper that did not echo the petition organized by the animal rights party demanding "retirement" for the elephants. The expression "retirement" did not even seem shocking […] If you read the articles there comes a time when you do not know if they are talking about undocumented immigrant field workers or animals […] We might think that these are simply journalists' subconscious metaphors […] The fact is that culture is made of metaphors. That is why we must ask ourselves if the whole animalistic tendency is not, in itself, the politicisation of a metaphor.

And: Seen within the timeframe of centuries, the development of the productive capacities of humanity tends to be translated into ideological forms ever more empathetic towards animals. From the deified beast, hostile and alien, we passed on to the animal-machine that relieves hunger and the burden of work and ultimately to the "experience" of the country school. Broadly speaking, the progress of the transforming capacity of the species extends our moral horizon, preparing humanity so that it can understand itself as part of a greater natural metabolism that only it can do self-consciously.

The fracture between humanity and nature cannot be healed without overcoming the fracture that sustains and divides our own species. Instead, an increasingly inhuman capitalism, proposes to "humanize" pets and animals. However this communion with nature cannot advance. The fracture with nature cannot be overcome without overcoming the fracture that sustains and divides our own species.

When they tell us about injured elephants and battered pets, do not forget that the real "elephant in the room", the cause of a thousand and one disasters that the media seem not to see, is called capitalism. And it is not a fable.

https://libcom.org/blog/behind-elephants-class-struggle-28042018

The elephant in the room may be capitalism (or its mutation), yes, but, here, again the elephant is taken as a metaphor. Capitalism is not the real animal. The real elephant is dead, just as the pre-industrial look we humans had for animals and animals for humans is also dead. No one died in the road accident, the bloggers say, when there is actually one body dead, depicted however as "only an elephant"; that is, only an animal, and as such, inferior to humans. What the bloggers imply here is precisely what Gramsci did not want in his letter: to substitute one metaphor for another. There will be no "overcoming the fracture that sustains and divides our own species". It will not be, cannot be, not because there is no time, but simply, because the fracture between humans happened at the same time the dividing line between humans and animals came to be: more or less, right at the moment when Louis XVI of France, the Sun King, imposed his sovereign gaze over the dead body of a female elephant during the autopsy practised on the animal at La Ménagerie de Versailles in 1681.

Jacques Derrida brings the scene to us in *The Beast and the Sovereign* (2009, p. 296). He reads the co-presence of the monumental (dead) elephant, the physicians, and the diminutive king surrounded by his court as a tableau vivant. An "autoptical", or "autopsic" scene, in his words, where the sovereign gaze of the Sun King is imposed over the doctors, the animal, and the people – a sovereign, thoroughly heliopolitical gaze:

> [T]his optical, autoptical scene […] makes use of an absolute power over the beast with a view to seeing and knowledge, in the name, at bottom, of Enlightenment, but of light, always that of the Sun King, light that in the end never dissociates theoretical observation in the service of knowledge, here for example the optics of autopsy – [never dissociates it] from spectacle, theater, ceremony as representation, and representation as representation *of* the king (a double genitive again), both the spectacular representation given by the king, ordered by him, organized by him in view of himself, and the representation *of* the king that represents the king, that presents him, shows him in his portrait, or recounts him in action (p. 287)

Theatrically, spectacularly, and hierarchically displayed so as to make clear the absolute sovereignty of the King, the scene is an example, Derrida tells us, of how Louis XIV embodies in his persona what Ernst Kantorowicz, following on Edmund Plowden's 1571 legal reports written in England under Queen Elizabeth I, termed "the king's two bodies", the Body Politic and the Body Natural (Kantorowicz, 2016): a mirror-image conceptualization sprouting from the medieval understanding of the mystical body of Christ as both divine and human, moving on also to the secular, post-revolutionary states emerging at the end of the seventeenth-century. In recalling the autopsy Derrida opens a fissure in the assumed inevitability of the transfer of the Political Body (sovereign power, *dignitas*, and *autoritas*, a body not seen and immune to decay) from the Natural Body of one sovereign to the next, a Natural Body subjected to deformities, infirmities, and ultimately, death. He underscores the scopic machinery of death that creates the illusion of sovereignty of man's dominion of animals, nature, and humans.

The massive and unsustainable use of animals by men, exemplified in its kernel in the autopsy scene witnessed by Louis XIV, extends itself, as Derrida tells us, through the age of Reason to the secular age of industrialization. It goes west, as Giacomo Marramao (2012) would say. The necroscopic gaze darting from the heliopolitical eyes of Louis XIV in 1681, a scene that takes in all its might the image of a mystical-political body with the sovereign as its head, moves onto its secular mutation after the great revolutions of the late 18th century: the American Revolution of 1776, and the French Revolution of 1789, the latter literally disposing of the head of the King. And they take an elephant with them: the captive elephant already imagined by Thomas Hobbes as the biblical and mythical Behemoth in 1681, the same year the autopsy of the elephant in the Menagerie took place: a Behemoth restrained by the Leviathan, as we know, the latter providing the path for the secular version of the state that, after the French Revolution, will carry intact the sovereign's Political Body.

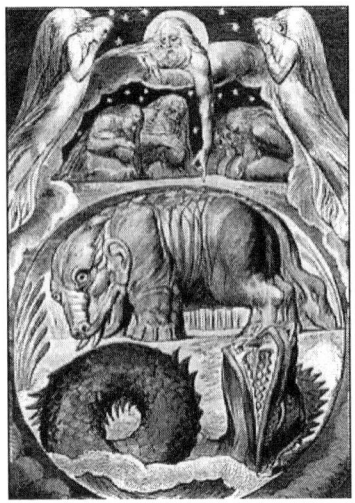

Behemoth and Leviathan watercolor by William Blake

The sovereign autopsic gaze identified by Derrida in the 1681 autopsy theater reigned supreme at the turn of the twentieth-century. Coinciding with the Codification of Law in Europe, Thomas Edison's presented in Coney Island spectacular moving images depicting the electric execution of an another female elephant, Topsy, the first in a series of films showing the electrocution of animals. Derrida's autopsic model, one always requiring the death of the animal, had become globalized. Edison's moving pictures, Kelly

Oliver reminds us, "inaugurated the electric chair as a form of execution in the United States. Moreover, the case of Edison (who invented both the electric chair and the first moving pictures, many of which were images of execution) makes manifest the connection between spectacle, animals, and the death penalty". (Kelly, 2012, p. 76).

Frames from the 1903, second short documentary film *Electrocuting an Elephant* produced by Edwin S. Porter or Jacob Blair Smith for the Edison Manufacturing Company.

The advent of urban electricity, the moving image, and the codification of Law, all human technical elements, take over the animal. We see – Oliver tells us – «how man's dominion over other animals is built on a model of sovereignty as necropsy that erects itself through the death of the animal» (*ibid.*). At the same time the codification of law in Europe becomes a reality, Edison uses and kills Topsy as an exemplary technical proposal for the electric chair – if the electricity can kill an elephant, so it will kill a man. There is no prioritizing here, not first the animals then humans, or first the humans then the animals, as the bloggers suggested when they stated that after all, the one dead body resulting from the accident was only that of an animal. Let animals be, tells Gramsci to his son: «The elephant's 'technical element', is his proboscis, and from an "elephantesque" point of view, he uses it marvelously» (1995, p. 381). No need to change anything on this front. Gramsci does not want the elephant to control anything, does not want the elephant to use man the way man uses the elephant. And, he does not take his son's proposals for the elephant metaphorically, but literally: in 1936 – he writes – history ends up not "as", but "with" the elephant's proboscis.

Visualized as an elephant's severed trunk, and considering Thomas Hobbes' Behemoth image for a lawless society in a natural state, in 1936 Gramsci's de-metaphorized figure of an elephant's severed proboscis could perhaps encapsulate the view of the ideologues of the Spanish Nationalist Christian Crusade against the communist peoples they called "hordes": masses as a partial object living in a state, the Spanish Republic, perceived without law and order; a state without a head, in fact: a mass with a non-subjective, acephalic drive, as perhaps Jacques Lacan would have it, ready to strike as a monstrous life-substance. Although, obviously, one could easily turn the image of the Behemoth associated with the headless and lawless masses around, and call the totalitarian regimes a Behemoth instead. Franz Neumann (1942) did precisely that in his book *Behemoth: The Structure and Practice of National Socialism*, where he sought to un-mask the authoritarian and autocratic face of the Nazi regime.

Neumann however, did not use a headless image of the Behemoth to describe the inner sinister workings of the Nazi regime, or any partial image. He had in mind the whole beast, which, as depicted by William Blake to illustrate *The Book of Job*, was imagined as an animal close to the hippopotamus, the rhinoceros, and, more often, a mammoth-like elephant. But George Bataille and André Masson did actually imagine an acephalic figure, in this case human, to describe the kind of (intellectual only?) action to be taken in the face of the state of things such as they were then. In the spring of 1936, while staying in a humble fisherman's house in the then tiny and remote coastal village of Tossa de Mar, in Catalonia. While Gramsci is in prison, we picture Masson and Bataille feeling happy, young, free, and powerfully restless while the thundering rambling of the upcoming war is creeping up in their backyard, they are in the little kitchen, and they imagine another world. They secretly conspire, or imagine themselves as conspirators. And in that same house, at that same kitchen table, they founded the journal *Acéphale*; they invoke Sade, Kierkegaard, and Nietzsche. They are ferociously religious in a new way, à la Kierkegaard; they proclaim themselves members of a new headless confederacy of the few, the smart, and the beautiful, those who are ready to undertake another kind of war; a Sadian-Nietzschean kind of war which, at this time and moment, even given the Marxist-Communist leanings of Bataille and Masson, could easily have fallen on the side of social-nationalist propaganda:

> It is necessary to produce and to eat: many things are needed that are yet nothing, and this is equally the case with political agitation.
> Before fighting to the bitter end, who thinks to leave his place to men that it is impossible to look upon without feeling the need to destroy them? But if nothing could be found beyond political activity, human greed would meet nothing but the void.
> WE ARE FEROCIOUSLY RELIGIOUS, and insofar as our existence is the condemnation of all that is recognized today, an internal requirement wants us also to be imperious.
> What we are undertaking is a war (Bataille, 1936).

The über-political statement in the manifesto («if nothing could be found beyond political activity, human greed would meet nothing but the void»), however, is quickly tempered. There is a move away from reason, from «the world of the civilized and its light», as well as an embracing of the quotidian, the pleasurable little things the house, the kitchen, the music and the sea provide:

> I am writing in a small cold house in a fishing village; a dog has just barked in the night. My room is next to the kitchen of André Masson, who is moving happily about and singing [...] It is time to abandon the world of the civilized and its light. It is too late to want to be reasonable and learned, which has led to a life without attractions. Secretly or not, it is necessary to become other, or else cease to be [...] Human life is defeated because it serves as the head and reason of the universe. Insofar as it becomes that head and reason it accepts slavery. If it isn't free, existence becomes empty or neuter, and if it is free, it is a game. The earth, as long as it only engendered cataclysms, trees, and birds was a free universe; the fascination with liberty became dulled when the earth produced a being who demanded necessity as a law over the universe. (Bataille, 1936, p. ????).

Like Gramsci the Sardinian did in his letter to Delio, Masson and Bataille, the Parisian cosmopolitans, imagine a figure closer to the Behemoth than to the Leviathan. There is a flow of energy here; of testosterone, of youthful male bonding. Of exuberance and excess. Energy is pouring right and left, and ever so literally. There is an excess of energy just when Europe is falling. Just when opposing the Behemoth, Giacomo Marramao reminds us, the Leviathan, that old Hobbesian paradigm of order sanctioned by the Peace of Westphalia, was starting to be felt not only «problematic in its single aspects or implications but in its very principle of construction». Marramao writes in *The Passage West*:

> The destiny of the 'mortal god', that is, of that 'jewel' of the *ius publicum europaeum* represented by the modern state-form is, in reality, inscribed in its very genesis. This is something Carl Schmitt had clearly seen and tried desperately to combat. The entropy of the Leviathan has its distant origin in the eternal contest between Earth and Sea: the opening up of the oceans determined by the process of insulating England in the Elizabethan era [...] [today we are facing] *another scene* [...] the falling away of that border [*confine*] between the *inside* and the *outside* that constituted the essential presupposition of the logic and function of the state. In the era of the 'finite world' (Valéry) and the planetary 'spatial revolution' (Schmitt), there is no *katechon* that appears able to check the inexorable decline of the Leviathan (2012, p. 94).

But entropy always requires at least two elements – in this case the Leviathan in relation to the Behemoth –, each element carrying a certain amount of (thermo-dynamic) energy grouped as/in microstates. Entropy is a direct measurement of the probability of displacement of each element's microstates into the other. And entropy, being called the "arrow of time", requires time, a particular direction for time. An arrow flying from 1681 in 1936, from Hobbes and Louis XIV to the Revolutions, from Benjamin Franklin in 1751 to Thomas Edison in 1903, and from Edison to Franco, Mussolini, Hitler, the Holocaust, and the hydrogen bombs. Entropy towards the Behemoth was already inscribed in the very genesis of the Leviathan, as Marramao notes. And from 1936-1945, and most precisely, after the advent of the nuclear bombs, no *katechon,* and no Sovereign Body, will be able to really rein it in. From 1945 on, the political body of the sovereign will, like the natural body, also be exposed to finitude. Not because there is no head anymore – who could really acknowledge today's chiefs of state as Heads? –; but because we have no elephant. Human life can now not even have a longing for clairvoyance. The excess of energy released by the H-Bombs forever killed the beast, poked its eyes out. Man will not "see" himself anymore in the animal's eyes – in any kind of light.

Right before the wear, Masson and Bataille's demanded, «to abandon the world of the civilized and its light»; to leave the lot of human life formed by those who see nothing, who exist with their "poked out eyes":

> When a few days ago I was in this kitchen with Masson, sitting with a glass of wine in my hand while he, suddenly imagining his own death and that of his kin, his eyes fixed, suffering, almost crying out that death had to become an affectionate and passionate death, crying out his hatred for a world that made weigh even on death its worker's hand, already I could no longer question that the lot and the infinite tumult of human life are open not to those who exist like poked out eyes, but to those who are like clairvoyants, carried away by an upsetting dream that could not belong to them (Bataille, 1936).

Their wish, however, will remain unfulfilled. At the end, killing the beast killed also the sovereign, a literal fact displayed almost like a joke when in 2012 the then King of Spain Juan Carlos I killed an elephant on a hunting trip in Botswana, Africa. He had a picture taken of himself with his trophy, one of many.

Photograph: Target Press/Barcroft Media

This particular one, however, was leaked in 2014 at the height of the economic crisis that choked the population, after the King was accidentally hurt in another hunting trip in Africa. It enraged the population. Juan Carlos abdicated that same year, a cloud of scandals and corruption casting over him. Reports Giles Tremet:

> While ordinary Spaniards cope with harsh austerity, recession and soaring unemployment, the country's royal family has been enjoying expensive hunting trips, one of which resulted in King Juan Carlos ending up in hospital [...] The 74-year-old monarch's fall in a park in Botswana provided an excuse for Spanish newspapers, who normally treat their royal family with kid gloves, to plaster their pages with photos of the king standing proudly in front of a dead elephant [...] The king's hunting trip, which officials described as private, has caused a storm of angry comment from animal lovers and those wanting to know how much it had cost (2012).

While King Juan Carlos abdicated over his son to avoid further damage to the monarchy, this time the sacral Political Body did not transfer its sovereignty over the new King's Natural Body, now that of Felipe VI of Spain. Three hundred years after the autopsy done in La Ménagerie, there seems to be no head, no beast, no eyes, no sovereign body in Spain – or in Europe, really. No katechon. Not even an autopsic gaze now. Not even a proboscis, detached or not. Not even a tusk, it seems. Only pure, elemental greed, of the kind reported in the news in 2013:

> More than 300 years after its death, a pet elephant that once belonged to King Louis XIV has been attacked by a would-be ivory poacher [...] The African elephant, whose skeleton stands in the anatomy gallery of the museum in the Jardin des Plantes was given to the Sun King by the king of Portugal in 1668. It lived in the zoo of Versailles Palace until its death in 1681 (Samuel, 2013, p. ???).

In 1946, after the war, after the dropping of the bombs, Bataille wrote:

> The living organism, in a situation determined by the play of energy on the surface of the globe, ordinarily receives more energy than is necessary for maintaining life; the excess energy (wealth) can be used for the growth of a system (e.g., an organism); if the system can no longer grow, or if the excess cannot be completely absorbed in its growth, it must necessarily be lost without profit; it must be spent, willingly or not, gloriously or catastrophically.

Today, transformed into greed, the excess of energy man took not only to kill the elephant, but also to pillage her tusk, will not be able to sustain the King's two bodies any longer. Today, sovereignty, it seems to me, can no longer be incorporated. Life, gloriously or catastrophically, will most likely continue; perhaps riding the arrow of time. But, also most likely, it will not be in the form of human life.

References

Bataille G. (1988). The Meaning of General Economy. In: *The Accursed Share. Essays on General Economy.* Vol 1.

Consumption. New York: Zone Books (Transl. of *La Part Maudite*. Paris: Editions de Minuit, 1967).
Bataille G. (2001). *Destruction: A Reader*, ed. by M. MacQuillan. New York: Routledge.
Berger J. (1998). How to Live With Stones. An Open Letter to Subcomandante Marcos in the Mountains of Southeast Mexico. http://articles.latimes.com/1998/jan/04/books/bk-4703
Berger J. (2009). *Why we look at Animals*. London: Penguin Books.
Castillo A. (2015) *Transmodernity*, 5.1: 142-58.
Cometa M. (2016). Non-finito. Antonio Gra*msci's Infrapolitical Writing*. https://infrapolitica.com/2016/04/05/non-finito-antonio-gramscis-infrapolitical-writing-by-michele-cometa/
Cometa M., A Conversation with Alberto Moreiras Regarding the Notion of Infrapolitics.
Derrida J. (2009). *The Beast and the Sovereign*. Vol. 1. Chicago: University of Chicago Press.
Gramsci A. (1994). *Letters from Prison*, ed. by F. Rosengarten. Transl. by R. Rosengarten.Vol. 2. New York: Columbia University Press.
Kantorowicz E. (2016). *The King's Two Bodies: A Study in Medieval Political Theology*. With an Introduction by C. Leyser and Preface by W. Chester Jordan. Princeton: Princeton University Press.
Kelly O. (2012). See Topsy 'Ride The Lightening': The Scopic Machinery of Death. *The Southern Journal of Philosophy*, Spindel Supplement, 50:7-94.
Lacan J. (1962). IX-Séminaire du 28 mars 1962. http://gaogoa.free.fr/Seminaires_HTML/09-ID/ID28031962.htm
Marin L. (1988). *Portrait of a King: Louis XIV*. Transl. by M. Hjort. Basingstoke: Palgrave MacMillan. Reprinted Baltimore: Johns Hopkins University Press.
Marramao G. (2012). *The Passage West: Philosophy after the Age of the Nation State*. Afterword by A. Negri. Transl. by M. Mandarini. London-New York: Verso.
Neumann F. (1942). *Behemoth: The Structure and Practice of National Socialism*. London: Victor Gollancz.
Samuel H. (2013). King Louis XIV's pet elephant attacked with chainsaw. Paris, 10:53PM BST 31 Mar 2013
https://www.telegraph.co.uk/news/worldnews/europe/

france/9964090/King-Louis-XIVs-pet-elephant-attacked-with-chainsaw.html

Tremlett G. (2012). Spain's King Juan Carlos under Fire over Elephant Hunting Trip. The Guardian, Sun 15 Apr 2012 09.30 EDT, https://www.theguardian.com/world/2012/apr/15/spain-king-juan-carlos-hunting

Humberto González Núñez

NEITHER PEOPLE NOR MULTITUDE
Posthegemony and the End of the Politics of Representation

> This is the limit of an era, which was the era of the representation of a meaning […]. We have exhausted the schemas of progress and of the progressive unveiling of truth. In this sense, History is indeed finished, or finite, and "finitude" opens another history […]. How are we to let it be seen that meaning exposes itself as impenetrable, and exposes us to this density? With what figure? By definition – that is, by the absencing of the ending (finition) – there will not be only one
>
> Nancy, 1997, pp. 83-84.

In the political thought, Paolo Virno offers us a decisive articulation of one of the fundamental conceptual confrontations within the history of Western political thought – the people and the multitude. There is no denying, as Virno perceptively indicates, «that the choice between "people" and "multitude" was at the heart of the practical controversies… and of the theoretical-philosophical controversies of the seventeenth century» (2004, p. 21). And, furthermore, the consequences of this conflict have left a significant impact on the structure of both our political thought and action. There are, according to Virno, two key factors that demonstrate the importance of this conflict for our contemporary political thought. The first central determination is the fact that the encounter between these two political figures resulted in a clear victor—the people. Even a casual glimpse of the history of Western politics would show that, in the modern epoch, the notion of the people has become the main referent for all political theorization and action. There would be no possible understanding of the modern republics without the decisive notion of the people.

Hence, there is no denying that the concept of the people has become the decisive and hegemonic figure for understanding the constitution of the public sphere.

The second critical determination concerns the vanquished or defeated figure of the political—the multitude. Following Virno's genealogy of the political, this defeat became even more consolidated by the following fact: «In describing the forms of associative life and of the public spirit of the newly constituted great States, one no longer spoke of multitude, but of people» (2016, p. 21). Again, this fundamental consequence of the decisively modern conflict of political thought and action can easily be confirmed by considering the history of Western politics. If we look at the constitution of modern States, then it is clear that we can find no clear reference to the multitude, especially when compared to the notion of the people. The various official documents and institutions do not consider themselves as acting on behalf of the multitude. Rather, the people constitute these institutions. In this sense, the multitude has been almost entirely effaced from our modern political lexicon. Only the people seem to be of relevance for an analysis of political phenomena.

It is at this point that we arrive to Virno's intervention within the debate concerning the people and the multitude. Although he recognizes the historical and hegemonic victory of the people over the multitude, Virno is unconvinced that this victory is irreversible. Instead, he asks, «whether, today, at the end of a long cycle, the old dispute has not been opened up once again» (2004, p. 21). Rather than continuing to assume the hegemonic position of the people as the fundamental political category, Virno's question allows for a decisive reopening that allows us to reconsider the historical answer in favor of the people. In contrast to the historical preference for the people, Virno describes his position in the following manner: «I maintain that the concept of "multitude," as opposed to the more familiar concept of "people," is a crucial tool for every careful analysis of the contemporary public sphere» (*ibid.*). Given that the notion of the people has lost all effectiveness, both in theory and practice, of describing the reality of political phenomena, it is only be returning to the multitude that we are capable of articulating a critical position vis-à-vis politics.

Virno's genealogy of the political leads us back to two of the most important political philosophers of that time and that happens to coincide with the seventeenth century debate between the people and the multitude – Thomas Hobbes and Baruch Spinoza. In fact, it would be impossible to think through both the philosophical and political determinations of the people and multitude without, in some way or another, referring to the work of these thinkers. On the one hand, the notion of the people appears at the core of Hobbes' *Leviathan* and, on the other hand, the concept of the multitude appears at the center of Spinoza's considerations in the *Theological Political Treatise*. Virno's introduces this fundamental conflict between Hobbes and Spinoza as a way of further highlighting the debate. While the two figures appear in both Hobbes and Spinoza, they certainly appear in a different light or tone. On the one hand, Hobbes' characterization of the people/multitude couplet sides with the people as the only political figure capable of constituting a political State as opposed to the anarchic impulses of the multitude. While on the other hand, Spinoza's engagement with this couplet sides more with the multitude as those individuals who are capable of grouping together and provoke the demand for further democratization of political institutions and so on.

Given this context, it seems clear that Virno's project responds to the attempt of recuperating the democratic impulses of the multitude such as they appear in Spinoza (but also beyond him). For Virno, the potency of the multitude allows for a crucial intervention in the structures and procedures with which we approach, both theoretically and practically, the affairs of the public sphere. In fact, he goes as far as considering that perhaps the "multitude [is] seen as the last cry of social, political and philosophical theory (2004, p. 22). In other words, face to face with the history of political thought, which seems to have privileged the notion of the people as the fundamental political category capable of making sense of that which takes place in the *polis*, the multitude appears perhaps as the last opportunity to produce a decisive shift that will be able to do justice to our current historical epoch. While Virno's claim that the multitude might represent the last cry of a decisive social, political, and philosophical intervention might be considered to be an exaggeration, it nonetheless helps shed further clarity on the stakes of his philosophical project. Thus, Virno's project is an attempt to carve out the space in which the multitude could become the main referent of our political thought and action. Having offered a sketch of Virno's important political genealogy, I propose another political genealogy through the work of Reiner Schürmann. My intention is not simply to oppose Schürmann to Virno. Instead, I propose the confrontation between two *types* of political genealogies. On the one hand, I claim that, insofar as Virno solely considers the people and the multitude as the two fundamental figures of politics, his political genealogy can only take place within the realm of hegemony. In other words, Virno's attempt to recuperate the potency of the multitude "against" the hegemony of the concept of the people can only take place as a "counterhegemonic" strategy. I claim that, by remaining within the hegemonic field, Virno's political genealogy suffers from severe limitations. In contrast to this approach, I argue that Schürmann's political genealogy allows for a *posthegemonic* strategy, that is to say, a strategy that does not simply decide either for the people or the multitude, but that recognizes the historicity of these and other ontic political figures. By recognizing the historicity of these ontic figures, Schürmann's political genealogy allows for both the deconstruction of all economies of presence relying on this structure (which, in this case, would also include Virno's) and the posthegemonic affirmation of that which is not determined by hegemonic or counterhegemonic discourse, which is what Schürmann terms "the singularization to come". By attending to the singularization to come, it is a matter of recognizing the end of the epoch of a certain use of representation within political thought and practice such that another opening – another beginning – becomes possible.

II. Even a cursory glance at Schürmann's extensive *corpus* would reveal his insistent preoccupation with the way in which certain economies of presence are constituted and deconstructed. Relying on a framework that is highly indebted to the work of Martin Heidegger, Schürmann proposes an analysis of these economies of presence by paying particular attention to the historicity of being and the way in which certain historical determinations of being affect the way in which we conceive of both thought and practice, broadly construed, in determinate historical epochs. If we follow Schürmann's determination, then it appears that metaphysical and ontological referents such as the One (*Hen*), Nature (*Phusis/ Natura*), Consciousness, Subjectivity, and so on, order the way in which we experience and work through the phenomenality of what appears. In order to further clarify the influence that these referents hold over determinate historical epochs, Schürmann, in his earliest work, focuses on the way in which "symbols" form an essential part of our experience of phenomenality. Of course, symbols will be of the utmost importance to us given that the ontic political figures – such as the people and the multitude – appear as nothing other than symbols that take place through the process of figuration or representation.

Schürmann's earliest writings appear guided by the following question: What is a symbol? Symbols appear coextensive with phenomenality itself. In other words, anything that appears within the phenomenal realm appears as a symbol. The symbol seems to be essentially linked to the constitution of a thing. Without symbols, we would perhaps be unable to either act or think our way through the world. While the constitution of a symbol seems coextensive with the constitution of a thing, it would be incorrect to consider the symbol as a purely static or inert thing. Instead, Schürmann rightly points out that «The symbol makes one do» (1997). Schürmann gives key examples such as the various symbols that take place, for example, in rituals or ceremonies. One could think of religious symbols and the way in which they constitute a certain forme of life. The imperative of the symbol is quite simply: "Go and do." In other words, the symbol provokes and invokes a response in which both thought and action are solicited and brought to the fore.

Keeping in mind Schürmann's early considerations of symbols and the process of symbolization, we come to better understand his emphasis on the construction of economies of presence following principial referents. Perhaps the clearest illustration of this point appears in Schürmann's *Heidegger on Being and Acting: From Principles to Anarchy* (1897). In this important study, Schürmann begins what he will consider his genealogy of principle with the "puma-shaped city". In other words, he analyzes the way in which the appearance of a symbol, such as the puma, begins to constitute the fundamental structures, institutions, and order of a city. Hence, the puma is a symbol, following Schürmann's understanding of the term, which determines both the thought and practice of a society. For Schürmann, the symbol as a determination of thought and practice appears in two registers that are, in the final analysis, correlated: the *principium* and *princeps*. According to Schürmann, the *principium* would be «the foundation that provides reasons and…[the *princeps* would be] the authority that dispenses justice» (1897, p. 25). Thus, the symbol has now become the concrete articulation of the principle of both reason and justice and, in this sense, holds sway over the entire political understanding of a determinate society. The Puma offers a legitimation of both the ordering of society and the very enactment of force and power. Through this symbol, an entire society constructs its sense of self as well as all kinds of normative injunctions that help make sense of a community's being-with.

At this point in Schürmann's genealogy of principles, we come to realize the particular political importance of symbols. It is not only the case that symbols appear as that which determines the very norms through which the communal life of a society takes place. Rather, the process of symbolization seems to be at work in the very foundations of political philosophy itself. It would be a mistake to consider political philosophy as somehow entirely divorced from speculative thought. In fact, Schürmann offers us the provocative thesis that these two uses of philosophical discourse cannot be separated haphazardly. Rather, it is a matter of understanding their co-constitution. Hence, following his early work on symbols, Schürmann writes, «Traditional philosophies of action have consistently been supported by some philosophy of "Being"» (1978, p. 357). In fact, he tells us that the very inheritance given to practical philosophy by speculative thought is «Precisely the reference to the first» (1987, p. 39). In other words, the structure of henology, that is to say, the logic constructed on the basis of the one, appears as that which links together both speculative and practical philosophy at their core. The reference to the One can take many shapes to the point that the One has always been more than one. While Schürmann focuses primarily on the metaphysical or ontological Ones that have held sway through different epochs of Western philosophical thought, I would like to extend the scope of principial referents to the realm of the history of Western political thought such that we would have to consider the people, multitude, proletariat, worker, and so on, as other symbols or referents that have in one way or another have contributed to the construction of what we could consider political henologies.

While it might seem that our intention is simply to translate Schürmann's genealogy of principles from metaphysical or ontological terms to political ones, nothing could be farther from the case. In fact, Schürmann offers an important yet all too brief consideration of the role of ontic political figures in the constitution of political henologies in the following manner: «From Plato's philosopher-king to Machiavelli's prince, this *pros hen* reference defines the relations of the many subjects to the one leaders as it defines the relations of the many accidents to substance and, in general, of the secondary analogotes to prime analogotes» (1987, p. 40). In other words, it would not be an exaggeration to consider the various political figures that have appeared throughout the history of Western thought as aiding in the constitution of political henologies through a *pros hen* relation, that is, a relation towards the One. Although our intention is not simply that of translating Schürmann's genealogy of principles from metaphysical or ontological terms to political ones, we are trying to explicate what seems to be an undeveloped thread. Within the context of the present essay, it is curious that Schürmann traces a line that only stems from Plato's philosopher-king to Machiavelli's prince, which seems to leave the question entirely open as to whether other political figures, such as the ones that we have already mentioned could be considered as contributing to the institution of political henologies. Going beyond merely exegetical analysis, our answer to this open question in Schürmann's work responds in the affirmative. Hence, it is possible and also necessary to consider both Hobbes' Leviathan and Spinoza's multitude as ontic figures capable of constituting political henologies.

The question of the constitution of political henologies around ontic political figures leads us directly to the question of hegemony, which appears even more forcefully in Schürmann's great posthumous work, *Broken Hegemonies* (2003). In this later text, Schürmann appeals to his task as an analytic of ultimates (as opposed to the genealogy of principles that characterized *Heidegger on Being and Acting*. Perhaps one of the most decisive innovations of *Broken Hegemonies* is the introduction of "hegemonic fantasms" as a key concept for the analytic of ultimates. For Schürmann, the task of thinking the hegemonic fantasms that appear throughout the history of Western thought begins with a consideration of the particular relation that takes place between the two terms—hegemony and fantasms. In other words, following Schürmann's concise determination:

> A fantasm is hegemonic when an entire cultures relies on it as if it provided that in the name of which one speaks and acts. Such a chief-represented (*hegemôn*) is at work upon the unspeakable singular when it calls it a part of the whole; hegemonies transform the singular into a particular. They serve to say what is, to classify and inscribe (2003, p. 7).

We should already note a connection between Schürmann's earlier and later work. For the notion of hegemony and its link with the figure of the *hegemôn* establishes an immensely important relation with the figure of the *princeps*. In both cases, a particular ontic political figure helps consolidate the very constitution of an economy of presence that corresponds to particular determinations of thought and practice according to the principial or hegemonic referents that appear within specific historical epochs. These figures allow for no respite or outside; instead, they indicate to us what and how we have to be. In other words, there seems to be no possibility of twisting free from the determinations of a hegemonic fantasm once it has become the main referent of an entire culture or society.

Schürmann offers a further important innovation in the transition from *Heidegger on Being and Acting* to *Broken Hegemonies* with the explication of the notion of the *singular*. This key notion, which does not appear at all in *Heidegger on Being and Acting*, will appear as one of the most important breakthroughs in Schürmann's entire œuvre since it offers another way of thinking through the constitution of henologies through principial referents or hegemonic fantasms such that another relation to both politics is made possible. Schürmann's understanding of the singular appears directly as a result of thinking through one of the classic triadic structures of the entire history of Western philosophy, that is to say, the particular-universal-singular structure. While Schürmann links the particular and universal as determinations that appear within the constitution of hegemonic fantasms, his understanding of the singular, in contrast, offers us a glimpse into that which seems to escape the process of subsumption that constitutes hegemonic discourse. Schürmann's analytic of ultimates, then, is guided by a motivation that did not fully or clearly appear in his genealogy of principles, which is the task of working through the hegemonies we have inherited historically in order to carve out the space where something like a singular, that is to say, non-hegemonic or, following our own terminology, *posthegemonic* relation to both thought and action in politics and other domains of life or existence is possible.

Following the decisive shift made possible by Schürmann's genealogy of principles to the analytic of ultimates, we are able to return to the question of political philosophy, that is to say, political henology and their constitution via ontic political figures. In fact, Schürmann raises the question with the aide of a new terminology or vocabulary in order to describe the particular limitations of political philosophy. If Schürmann's earlier critique of political philosophy had to do with the fact that it had inherited the structure of speculative philosophy (i.e. henology), then his later critique seems to sharpen this critique by bringing into play the relationship between universality, particularity, and singularity. In other words, Schürmann suggests that political philosophers will suffer from the greatest naïveté insofar as they remain content with trying to reconcile universality and particularity, as if these two determinations exhausted the totality of political life. Instead, this kind of perspective can only take place with an oblivion or explicit erasure of that other key determination that appears in the context of the public sphere, that is to say, the singular. Thus,

Schürmann asks: «What if the common and the singular both bind us—then is it not rather that we inhabit a ravaged site? Might the singular be lodged within a truth other than the common? How, then, is one to extract it from the common» (2003, p. 16). Schürmann's question allows us to glimpse at the "double bind" that determines our contemporary epoch—between commonality and singularity. However, while contemporary political philosophy have ventured into an explication of commonality whether through the figure of the multitude or other political figures, the case remains that there has still been an inattentiveness to the singular and the way in which it seems to interrupt, suspend or escape hegemonic discourse. Perhaps something essential for our political thought and practice is at stake in thinking through the singular and the singularization to come, which, according to Schürmann, is never fully managed or administrated by hegemony, but, instead, appears as the undertow of every hegemonic fantasm. Perhaps this attention to the singular would open the possibility for another kind of political thought and practice—one that we have termed posthegemonic.

III. If we return to the initial Hobbesian scene offered to us by Virno—people versus multitude—then we would notice that, following both Schürmann's genealogy of principles and analytic of ultimates, the terrain has fundamentally and decisively shifted. In other words, it seems difficult, if not almost impossible, to salvage either the ontic figure of the people *or* the multitude as referents for our political thought and practice. This difficulty is expressed by way of two main reasons. The first reason takes place through a consideration of the historicity of these ontic figures, which appears as a direct consequence of a genealogy of principles. In other words, these figures appeared at a particular moment in history—modernity—and operated as an important way to make sense of the public sphere and the ways in which politics took place in it. However, if we are to continue elucidating both the historicity of these figures and the historicity that we are in or that we ourselves *are*, then we would have to recognize that their validity for guiding our political thought and practice cannot occur once and for all, but must also be submitted to the ravages of time. Once we recognize the way in which these ontic figures are constituted historically, then it can no longer be a matter of simply retaining them at all costs—as the last cry of social, political, and philosophical theory as Virno claims. Instead, it would be a matter of thinking through the way in which these figures appear within a particular historical conjuncture through a singular that is never fully given, but expresses itself as the undertow of all hegemonic figuration. This last point opens up to the second reason, which would take place with an explicit consideration with the singular as that which is not subsumable to hegemonic determinations. In other words, if we recognize that there is something that is not fully capable of being submitted to the hegemonic determinations that have been at work in our modern political thought and practice, then would it not be the case that an attention to this singularization to come would open a rift such that an entirely other relationship not only to politics, but also history and existence?

By attending to these considerations, we have revealed what we could consider a general hypothesis concerning the end or closure of the epoch of the politics of representation. Following this general hypothesis, it would be a matter of asserting that it is no longer possible to rely on principial referents or hegemonic fantasms that appear in the guise of ontic political figures to guide our political thought and practice. In other words, it can no longer be a matter of claiming to be either for the people or the multitude. However, it is also clear that it is not a matter of being totally against or in favor of political figuration. Instead, the task seems to be to engage in a critical-deconstructive relation that recognizes the historicity of our political figures so as to not reduce all political thought and practice to henological discourse. Another possible affirmation – a posthegemonic one – is possible by following the diremption at stake in all political henologies, that is to say, in the notion of a singularization to come. Rather than a mystifying doctrine, this attention to singularity indicates nothing other than the following: we cannot remain content with the simple affirmation that all political thought or action can be reduced to an attention towards either this or that ontic political figure. Instead, an attention to the singular would reveal the double bind that constitutes our very condition: the emergence of political figures can take place within the incessant movement of history such that we will never be done with figures, which is perhaps what Schürmann would understand by natality, and the historicity of these figures indicates a something else that can never fully be subsumed under these referents and, nonetheless, appears crucial to all political thought and action—the singular which would appear as a result of a confrontation with what Schürmann calls mortality. By heeding to the incessant interaction of these two poles that seem to constitute our ravaged site, it seems that a posthegemonic politics would declare the following two demands, which perhaps are just two ways of expressing a single thought: posthegemony would be a "politics without figures", that is to say, a politics of always "more than one" figure.

References

Badiou A. (2016). *What Is A People?* New York: Columbia University Press.
Nancy J.-L. (1997). *The Gravity of Thought*. Atlantic Highlands, NJ: Humanities Press International.
Schürmann R. (1978). Questioning the Foundations of Practical Philosophy. *Human Studies*, 1, n. 1: 357-368.
Schürmann R. (1987). *Heidegger on Being and Acting.From Principles to Anarchy*. Bloomington, IN: Indiana University Press.
Schürmann R. (1997). Symbolic Difference. *Graduate Faculty Philosophy Journal*, 19, 2-1: 9-38.
Schürmann R. (2003). *Broken Hegemonies*. Bloomington, IN: Indiana University Press.
Virno P. (2004). *A Grammar of the Multitude. For an Analysis of Contemporary Forms of Life*. New York: Semiotext(e).
Virno P. (2016). *What is People?*. New York: Columbia University Press.

MADDALENA CERRATO
BEYOND THE COMMUNITY
The Refugee as Infrapolitical Problem

> Tu lascerai ogne cosa diletta più caramente; e questo è quello strale che l'arco de lo essilio pria saetta. Tu proverai sì come sa di sale lo pane altrui, e come è duro calle lo scendere e 'l salir per l'altrui scale[1]
>
> Dante, *Paradiso* XVII, 55-61

Here, the term "refugee" stands for a whole problematic field rather than a mere juridical category. It is the field of the timeless questions of exile to which Dante's epigraph points. Refugee stands as the title for a field where a number of distinct although contiguous – and often treated as interchangeable-figures dwell, from the stateless to the displaced person, from the fugitive to the *apatride*, from the exiled to Here, the term "refugee" stands for a whole problematic field rather than a mere juridical category. It is the field of the timeless questions of exile to which Dante's epigraph points. Refugee stands as the title for a field where a number of distinct although contiguous – and often treated as interchangeable – figures dwell, from the stateless to the displaced person, from the fugitive to the *apatride*, from the exiled to the asylum seeker, to the guest. The problem of refugees from time to time has become front-page news. It imposes itself as an emergency. Journalistically speaking, it is indeed an emergency both in the sense of a dramatic and alarming situation as well as in the etymological sense of being something emerging. Politically

---

[1] You shall leave everything you love most dearly: /this is the arrow that the bow of exile shoots first. You are to know the bitter taste/ of others' bread, how salty it is, and know how hard a path it is for one who goes /descending and ascending others' stairs.

and philosophically, though, talking about an emergency of the question of refugees does not seem quite appropriate. This is clearly not because it is not a dramatic and alarming question, rather because considering it emerging would be a stretch. In *The Origins of Totalitarianism*[2], Hannah Arendt sets World War I as the turning point that prompted the question of refugees to emerge as mass phenomenon and a true political crisis. At this point, the question by far should have gone beyond the status of "emergency" and should have acquired that of an already emerged, constant, and persistent issue. On the other hand, the figure of refugee keeps presenting itself as a sign of unpredictable and extra-ordinary circumstances, a paroxysm of the novelty of the times, as an emblem of the new intellectual challenges that contemporary political thought needs to face. And this would suggest that the question rather than being emerging, is still submerged, immersed, and sunk in conceptual ambiguities that exceed the legal-political order.

After Arendt, among others, Giorgio Agamben, Werner Hamacher, and Jacques Derrida have reopened the discussion in interesting and related ways. Here, what I am going to do to contribute to such a theoretical debate is to try to detach the question of the refugee from the chiliastic announcement of the decline of the nation-state and so, to frame it as an infrapolitical problem. As we will see, these two moves are inherently tied one to the other and both call for a topological analysis of the question of the refugee and its relation to the model of the nation-state.

1. Toward a topology of the refugee

In "We Refugees" Giorgio Agamben writes: «The refugee should be considered for what he is, that is, nothing less than a border concept that radically calls into question the principles of

---

2   Arendt is the first to discuss the inherent complexity and ambiguity of the question surrounding the figure of the refugee in her brief article "We Refugees" (1943), first, and then in the ninth chapter of *The Origins of Totalitarianism* (1948) "The Decline of the Nation-State and the End of the Rights of Man."

the nation-state and, at the same time, helps clear the field for a no-longer-delayable renewal of categories» (1995, p. 117). Here, Agamben is referring to the renewal of the state-nation-territory triad supporting the modern concept of citizenship as principle of the juridical and political subjectivity of men. Such a renewal would become urgent in the wake of the "decline" of the nation-state. After almost fifty years, Agamben is revamping Arendt's perspective from *Origins of Totalitarianism*, though he conjugates it with the theoretical optimism -which there already Arendt had abandoned- of the conclusion of "We Refugees." In the 1943 article, she looked at refugees as the vanguard of the European political state of affairs:

> Refugees driven from country to country represent the vanguard of their people – if they keep their identity. For the first time Jewish history is not separated but tied up with that of all other nations. The comity of European peoples went to pieces when, and because, it allowed its weakest member to be excluded and persecuted (p. 119).

In the same way, Agamben assigns to refugees the task of instructing political philosophy as to the right path for rethinking its foundational category of community after an epochal historical crisis:

> in the context of the inexorable decline of the nation-state and the general corrosion of traditional legal-political categories, the refugee is perhaps the only imaginable figure of the people in our day. At least until the process of the dissolution of the nation-state and its sovereignty has come to an end. The refugee is the sole category in which it is possible today to perceive the forms and limits of *a political community to come* (1995, p. 114).

In his perspective, the ultimate aim, and what one could call a critical eschatology of questioning the legal and political paradoxes that the figure of the refugee entails, is nothing less than «to reconstruct our political philosophy beginning with this unique figure» (*ibid.*). When the decline of nation-state sovereignty condemns the traditional forms of political subjectivity and challenges the stability of community as horizon for political action, the contradiction embodied by the refugee – who instead of enacting the relevance of the rights of men, shows their very limits – is called on to show the way to a conceptual renewal of the category of community beyond the perspective of the national politics of modernity.

In this context, the essential theoretical move I want to put forward is the passage from this historical chiliastic perspective of the "decline of the nation-state" to a topological perspective. This is not to minimize the importance of an historical perspective, and even less to overlook the historicity of the political categories called into question. Rather, my goal is to analyze those aporias and contradictions inherent to our historical and political dwelling that the figure of refugee highlights, free from the drive to overcome them dialectically in order to recover and protect community's integrity. This move allows me to consider the refugee not only or not properly as a political question, rather as an infrapolitical one. This means trying to untangle the discussion of the refugee from the goal of solving the juridical aporia represented by *The Rights of the Man and the Citizen*, as well as from the venture into a complete renewal of political categories as such. Of course, this does not mean denying the important political implications of such a matter, rather it points out the fact that it also belongs to an existential field that exceeds the limits of political-juridical subjectivity and highlights the inherent limits of its foundational concept of community.

A topological analysis is one that considers historical political categories and principles, as well as their contradictions and aporia, as places, or sites on the ground of historical existence within and in excess of which human beings dwell and experience life. In my perspective, the theoretical gesture that gives priority to the analysis of existence as an attempt at mapping the historically given symbolic places of human dwelling, at inquiring into the contradictions that mark human experience represents the infrapolitical gesture *par excellence*. Thinking infrapolitically – thinking infrapolitics – means first of all questioning the seizing of existence by modern subjectivity, which means questioning the pretension of exhausting and saturating the topology of human existence and experience through the framework offered by the internal articulation of modern subjectivity into a political, ethical, and gnoseological subject.

This theoretical move from the historical chiliastic perspective of the "decline of the nation-state" to a topological perspective is modelled on the fundamental critical gesture of Reiner Schürmann's monumental work *Broken Hegemonies* (2003). There, Schürmann presents a topological analysis of the *ultimates* – the ultimate principles that bear the normative order – where he shows how every thetic gesture of instauration of a normative order able to subsume and organize phenomenic reality always already entails the negation of the irreducibility of the singular existence. His analysis reveals the permanence of a non-subsumable excess behind any hegemonic constitution. An irreducible impulse to singularization persists behind the instauration of common representations that organize the normative horizon of community. Human existence is marked by two different impulses. The first is the impulse that Schürmann calls, along with Arendt, "natality". Natality is the normative impulse to structure reality through principles, norms, and common representations that find a direct expression in the predicative function of language. On could say that this is the "immortalizing" drive toward ontotheology. The second the impulse that Schürmann calls, along with Heidegger, being-toward-death or "mortality". This is the impulse of withdrawal of the singular, this is, of the disperse object of passion that remains unnamed and that without a title offers itself only in *deixis*. They do not generate a mere opposition, nor a dialectic contradiction, rather a double bind that constitutes the tragic condition of human existence. Every hegemonic principle – every normative theticism – cannot but institute a fantasmic hegemony built on the negation of the tragic condition of existence, on the denial of the co-belonging of normative impulse and transgressive impulse, natality and mortality, community and singularity. Schürmann's topology strives to recover such an originary tragic tension to reveal the deep mechanism that governed the emergency and destitution of normative principles, or as he says "the history of *norms*".

I understand this term [norms] in its strongest sense, the sense in which it names the authoritative representation that serves, during a given linguistic era, to constitute the *phenomenality of phenomena* and thereby to *legitimize all theoretical and practical rules*. In the normative sense, a fantasm cannot be exhausted in regulatory representations. It designates the sovereign principle to which the professional philosopher refers all laws of knowledge and acting, but which in turn cannot be referred to anything else, the principle that serves as the ultimate reason for all generic principles, the trans-regional canon for all regional canons. (2003, p. 6, *my emphasis*).

It is such a tension that explains how those "ultimates", which constitute the "phenomenality of phenomena" and "legitimize all theoretical and practical rules", end up dissolving themselves, empting out their own authority torn apart by a contradiction that they had negated yet always already carried.

Here, I would like to bring into play Schürmann's analysis with respect to the relationship between the issue of the refugee and the decline of the nation-state to show how hegemony of the model of the nation-state already contained the seeds of its decline, or better yet the contradiction that causes its dissolution, and this is what the figure of refugee reveals.

2. *The refugee and the topology of the nation-state*

The principle that generates and guides the nation-state, this is its *arché*, is nationalism understood, along with Ernst Gellner, as «primarily a political principle, which holds that the political unit and the national unit should be congruent» (1983, p. 1). Borrowing the terms of Schürmann's analysis, one can say that nationalism is the authoritative principle that organizes political phenomenality in the modern political order, offering an endless supply of signification and normative measures to which political representations, praxes, and ideals are to be referred. In this perspective the figure of the refugee reveals itself as the embodiment of the transgressive impulse to singularization undermining any normative construction. It is the excess that unveils the fantasmic nature of the hegemonic principle of nationalism and challenges the way it presents itself in order to preserve its authority, beyond any critical reach. «Nationalism sees itself as a natural and universal ordering of the political life of mankind» (p. 47). This way, in the relationship between refugee and nation-state, we should not read the index of the latter's decline rather a manifestation of the tragic condition of existence that has in the political community its *topos*, its site *par excellence*.

The refugee is – as Agamben suggested – in a sense as a border concept, or better, as the inherent limit to the community as possible site of totalization. It unveils as empty the community pretension of being (destined to be) the site for the congruence and the indistinctiveness between the political and the cultural, the latter understood as coincidence of the ethic and the ethnic. This is the limit of community as the symbolic place of the legitimation of political subjectivity, as well as the ethical- political *tout court*.

The title of refugee represents the paradox of a post-hegemonic title. This is a title that, instead of marking a particular position within the normative order, marks the impossibility of the latter to be exhaustive. It unveils the political inability to saturate existence. In *Who's Afraid of Philosophy? The Right to Philosophy 1*, Derrida writes:

> Questions of title and right always have a *topological* dimension. No institution does without a symbolic place of legitimation, even if assigning this place can be overdetermined at the intersection of empirical and symbolic, physico-geographic and ideal givens within a homogeneous or heterogeneous space (2002, p. 9).

In the case of the nation-state model, the institution of the state chooses as the symbolic place of its legitimation the ethnic community and tries to make it coincide with the empirical place of a certain physico-geographic territory. Gellner captures this very clearly in his second formulation:

In brief, nationalism is a theory of political legitimacy, which requires that ethnic boundaries should not cross political ones, and in particular, that ethnic boundaries within a given state – a contingency already formally excludes by the principle of its general formulation – should not separate the power-holders from the rest (1983, p. 1). Nationalism founds the legitimacy of the sovereignty and the territoriality associated with the modern state since the Peace of Westphalia on the demand for such a boundary coincidence, and on the implicit topology of community that in exchange turns out to be politicized, this means made explicit, overdetermined, and structured in reality. Indeed, as Carlo Galli underscores, not only is it «the space of the implicit spatial representations in and through which political thought supports itself» (2010, p. 11), but at the same time «politics arranges itself in space and arranges space itself not only in thought but politicizing, producing and structuring space in reality» (p. 12). So, not only the nation-state is grounded in a certain topological representation of the ethnic-cultural community that stays right at the intersection of empirical and symbolic, but at the same time such an ethnic-cultural community finds itself politically overdetermined and topologically structured on the basis of the principle of nationalism.

Nationalism as the principle that establishes political legitimacy from and on the ethnic community, initiates a complex (and somewhat circular) thetic-normative operation that works on two levels. On the one hand, nationalism establishes the norm for political legitimacy, which means the principle of legitimacy for the constitution of the state and law as much as the principle of universal equivalence for political units. On the other hand, it institutes as well the ethnic community as the principle of pre-legitimation *a posteriori*. This is because, as Derrida (2002) explains, the concept of legitimation is itself undermined by the fact that «it has no opposite. Nonlegitimacy can appear as such, be its signs ever so discreet, only in a process of prelegitimation» (p. 14). It is only in the institution of the community as ethnic community that the political community grounds its legitimacy, and also its topology, meaning the topology that organizes its law. The legitimacy of state sovereignty derives from its coincidence of the territoriality on which it is exercised with the community's topology, meaning with the sites of community dwelling. At the same time, not only is the title that identifies the belonging to the national community guaranteed by the state as institution, but the state institutions intervene conspicuously in building and delimiting the symbolic space of the ethnic community.

No nation possesses an ethnic base naturally, but as social formations are nationalized, the populations included within them, divided up among them or dominated by them are ethnicized – that is, represented in the past or in the future *as if* they formed a natural community, possessing of itself an identity of origins, culture and interests which transcends individual and social conditions (Balibar, 1991, p. 96).

The constitution of what Balibar calls the «fictive ethnicity» of the nation, as well as the imaginary of the nation – both of which are expressions of an artefactual primordialism – emerge performatively from state institutions everyday praxis and from the right implementation in the common space organized as extension of institutionalized family space.

The belonging to the national community legitimized the holder of institutional power, but only this very institution administers the topological dimension of the title and the right to such a belonging. At the same time, the national community is accomplished only in its identification with the state, which becomes once more reaffirmed in the synonymic relation in everyday language between the two components of the "nation-state" pair. The interplay between the belonging to the symbolic space of the national community and the belonging to the territory of the efficacy of the rule of law marks the topology of the nation-state as a paradoxal space and as the site of an essential disjunction always already signaled by the hyphen that separates at least as much as it unites state and nation. Such a disjunction indeed represents a constitutive paradox, rather than a sign of decline induced by the infamous threats globalization brought about. The constitutive paradox that marks the topology of the nation-state is what emerges in the conceptual ambiguity surrounding the question of the refugee. Thus, in order to understand the problematic field to which we referred through the title of refugee, one needs to look at the contradictions inherent to the institution of the community as ethnic community. And at the same time, in order to understand the genealogy of such contradictions, rather than to try to build a new horizon of legitimacy for the political community, it is worth looking at the figure of the refugee.

3. *Radical negativity of the title of refugee*

The title of refugee identifies a problematic field that is marked by an essential negativity, which ultimately is the radical negativity of singularity and mortality. An essential negativity seems indeed to concern every level, every aspect, every articulation of this matter. First of all, such a negativity marks the difference with respect to the figure of the migrant. In spite of all of the dreadful difficulties and dramatic conditions migrants go through, their symbolic position is tied to the hopeful positivity of a teleological perspective, to the idea of a new beginning, and to the generative productive impulse of "natality". Second, the radical negativity of the refugee marks the difference with respect to the position of so-called minorities, that is, the allogenic groups excluded in the process of building the ethnic primordialism of the national community but recognized this way. The negativity of the position of these groups is a dialectic negativity, that is the determinate negation serving the definition of the ethnic community, of citizenship, and of the internal mechanisms of distinction and exclusion. In this sense, minorities both retain a "positive negativity", and also boast a "negative positivity", since their exclusion is based on the constitution of an alternative ethnic community. On the one hand, minorities' negativity works to define those ethnic boundaries that political boundaries commit to respect. On the other, the constitution of an ethnic community as a minority by opposition to the national community confirms and perpetuates the same logic of identitary primorsialist subjectivation that generated its exclusion in the first place. This is the logic that supports the political legitimation based on the principle of nationalism even to the paroxysm of its autoimmunitarian manifestations[3].

The question of the refugee refers first of all to a matter of attributing titles and rights and we know – remembering Derrida's already quoted words – that «questions of title and right always have a *topological* dimension». The topology of the entire field of this question is extremely complex and has been the ground for an intense juridical debate for the last sixty years. I would like to suggest that this complexity is the consequence of the fact that the legitimation of the title and rights at stake is tied to a radically negative symbolical topology.

---

3   On this matter that I can not adequately discuss here, see for example Esposito (2010, 2012).

The four categories that inhabit the problematic field of the refugee and seem to fail in organizing and structuring it are: the asylum seeker, the refugee, the stateless (in Italian *apolide* and in French *apatride* with a significant etymological variety) and the internally displaced person. First, one needs to note that these are neither equivalent nor reciprocally alternative and exclusive categories, rather they are subject to multiple and controversial overlappings. According to the definition of the status of refugee included in the first article of the Geneva Convention of 1951:

As a result of events occurring before 1 January 1951 and owing to well- founded *fear* of being persecuted for reasons of race, religion, nationality, membership of a particular social group or political opinion, *is outside* the country of his nationality and is *unable* or, owing to such fear, is *unwilling* to avail himself of the protection of that country; or who, *not having a nationality* and being outside the country of his former habitual residence as a result of such events, is unable or, owing to such fear, is unwilling to return to it (my emphasis).

The negativity of the refugee – who is the asylum seeker at first – is the radical negativity of the exiled, expatriate, displaced person, *profugus*. A condition of risk and fear pushed the refugee outside the place of his/her dwelling, outside his/her being-at-home and toward an escape (*pro-fuga*) that is an indefinite departure, an undetermined and endless getting away. The "asylum seeker" is the title of those who aspire to a title either of "refugee" or "stateless" that could give them the right to an *asylum*, a Latin form coming from the Greek *asylon a - syle* (right to seizure) that as an adjective comes to signify «not subject to seizure by one's pursuers, or it may mean protection or freedom from such seizure» (*Black's Law Dictionary*, p. 159). The right to *asylum* is the right to a form of protection that was supposed to be a prerogative of the political community that instead now is the one threatening and/or expelling. Asking for *asylum* is the beginning of a process of pre-legitimation not from a symbolic place of legitimation, but rather from a condition of exclusion or expulsion from the symbolic originary place of the primordial national community. This means seeking a title that does not offer a place in a community rather a refuge, a shelter, a protection, that is, it is a title that marks neither an inclusion nor an exclusion (either internal or external) rather a status -provisional by definition- of guest. Once more Derrida: «A community (being-with, being-together, meeting, convened by convention) is always presupposed in the value of the word and concept 'title'» (2000, p. 15). In this sense, the title of refugee – as well as, with very little distinction, that of stateless and internally displaced persons – is a non-title. It is the title that signals the return to the proper name. It is the title that signals the absence and the impossibility of a title given the state of extraneousness and (symbolic and/or physical) exteriority to the political community. This is a status of double extraneousness, both with respect to the community of origin as well as to the one receiving. This means that ultimately it is the condition of alienation from the political community as such which is the condition of the one who broke the symbolic bond with the birthplace, with birth as a symbolic place of political legitimation.

The human being who has lost his place in a community, his political status in the struggle of his time, and the legal personality which makes his actions and part of his destiny a consistent whole, is left with those qualities which usually can become articulate in the sphere of private life and must remain unqualified, mere existence in all matters of public concern (Arendt, 1966, p. 301).

Arendt then explains "this mere existence" as «all that which is mysteriously given us by birth and which includes the shape of our bodies and the talents of our minds» (*ibid.*), meaning everything that concerns the law of diversity and infinite differentiation. However, that which at birth consigns us to the law of infinite differentiation challenging the principle of equivalence that holds the normative order is death. Birth brings us into a world of fantasmic taxonomies and consigns us to the order of common nouns, yet birth gives us also our proper name which is the only one that remains attached to us until death. Death – understood broadly as the threat or fear of death – is what breaks the tie with the community of birth, with birth as a principle of political action. Death leaves the refugee outside a place in the world that «makes opinions significant and actions effective» (p. 296), leaving him «in a situation where, unless he commits a crime, his treatment by others does not depend on what he does or does not do» (*ibid.*). At the same time, his birth, the "allogeny" with respect to the place that eventually welcomes him, maintains the refugee as foreigner, stranger, outsider with respect to the community *at home*.

Birth maintains the refugee attached to her mortal singularity and refuses to her the possibility of the – always fantasmic – community subsumption. The kind of protection to which she might gain access is not the positive protection of the right to have rights guaranteed by the belonging to the juridical community. It is instead a shelter from the fear of death that yet subsists and becomes the only (infra-)political determination of the refugee's existence. The fear of death pushes and maintains refugees in a condition of anomy that also condemns them to a *de facto* anonymity. Once the tie to the community is broken, the refugee loses not only the title and the social status, but the value of the proper name as ethnic and family tie. The name remains, though emptied out of any significance since it does not signal any longer the tie to the family, to ancestors, to descendants, and ultimately to the nation.

Going back to Schürmann's perspective, the condition of the refugee reveals the very existential double bind resulting from the irreconcilable contention between the singularizing force of death and the normative instituting power of birth. In the refugee condition, the tragic condition of existence makes itself visible. The figure of the refugee reveals what the community strives to negate. And, this would explain the general perception of the figure of the refugee as inherently uncanny and the treatment of his presence as undesirable. Benedict Anderson shows how the historical fortunes and the political efficacy of the model of national community depend to a great extent on its ability to secularize the religious thought's capacity to respond «to the obscure intimations of immortality, generally by transforming fatality into continuity [...] contingency into meaning» (2006, p. 11) in a new form of political imagination. The figure of the refugee brings fatality and contingency back and into the foreground. It shows the fragility of the ethnic tie, the dissolubility of the political pact, the instability of the rootedness in a territory, as it shows the impossibility of community to capture, subsume, and exhaust the possibility of singular existence in its norms. In this sense, it is also easy to understand from where the resistance to recognizing the status of refugee as permanent institution and where the attempt to keep treating the question as exception and emergency come.

Finally, the radical negativity is what determines the particular status of the refugee as guest as well. The refugee, and so the stateless and the displaced person, is not in the position of the foreigner with a name, a title, and a social status that – as Derrida has explained – who gets access to the right to hospitality as the result of a pact of reciprocal and conditional hospitality between sovereign nations. The refugee is the absolutely Other that summons the absolute or unconditional hospitality that does not respond to a right or a duty.

To put it in different terms, absolute hospitality requires that I open up my home and that I give not only to the foreigner (provided with a family name, with the social status of being a foreigner, etc...), but to the absolute, unknown, anonymous other, and that I give place to them, that I let them come, that I let them arrive, and take place in the place I offer them, without asking of them either reciprocity (entering into a pact) or even their names (2000, p. 25).

The topology of the refugee would be the negative topology of the threshold. Such a threshold rather than marking a border with the outside, signals the possibility of entering through the internal tragical fracture of political subjectivity into another dimension of the existence that one can call infrapolitical.

References

Agamben G. (1995). We Refugees. *Symposium* 49, 2: 114-119.
Anderson B. (2006). *Imagined Communities.* London-New York: Verso.
Arendt H. (1966). *Origins of Totalitarianism.* "A Harvest Book". New York: Harcourt:
Arendt H. (1994). We Refugee. In: *Altogether Elsewhere*: *Writers in Exile,* ed. by M. Robinson, London: Faber and Faber: 111-119.

Balibar E. (1991). *The Nation Form. Race, Nation, Class: Ambiguous Identities*. London-New York: Verso.
Derrida J. (2000). *Of Hospitality*. Stanford: Stanford University Press.
Derrida J. (2002). *Who is Afraid of Philosophy? Right to Philosophy*. Stanford: Stanford University Press.
Galli C. (2010). *Political Spaces and Global War*. Minneapolis-London: University of Minnesota Press. Gellner E. (1983). *Nations and Nationalism*. Ithaca, NY: Cornell University Press.
Schürmann R. (2003). *Broken Hegemonies*. Bloomington, IN, Indiana University Press.
Esposito R. (2012). *The Terms of the Political: Community, Immunity, Biopolitics*. Transl. by R.N. Welch. New York: Fordham University Press.
Esposito R. (2013). Community, and the Proper. *Special Issue: Angelaki*, 18/3: 83-90.

Peter Baker
POLITICS OF THE MULTITUDE
Seven Theses on Posthegemony

> Though the multitude initiates revolution too soon something goes wrong. What begins as immanence and liberation, as innovation and creativity, ends up as transcendence and normalization, as the state form and its *repressive apparatuses*.
>
> Jon Beasley Murray, *Posthegemony*

> [Even] its fiercest detractors from the left and right recognize that, today, anything substantial that is to be said about Europe and North America must deal and engage with the "populist moment".
>
> Íñigo Errejón. *Occidente en su momento populista*

This paper presents seven theses which attempt to elucidate the significance of certain contemporary debates on the question of populism from the perspective of what others have identified as the contemporary crisis of the political architectonics of modernity through the work of contemporary Italian theory, especially the work of Paolo Virno. It will argue, against the grain of some of the dominant forms of understanding the theory and practice of contemporary populisms today, that the theory of populism as we find it in the work of Ernesto Laclau and others is in fact a specific response to emerging conditions of political action, and not the attempt to restore earlier and outdated forms of political sovereignty linked to the nation state form. Despite its place as both a theory and practice of political action in our contemporary conjuncture "after the Leviathan", I suggest that the theory of populism as a theory of social and political action does not sufficiently explore the heart of the problem with which it is concerned; that is, the conditions which are given within the current configuration of capitalist relations which make action and reflection possible today. By taking a certain distance from the Laclauian theory of populism and accepting that there are areas of the human experience which are not reducible to politics as a field of action, we propose that the question over how contemporary conditions for action are given necessarily exceeds the political sphere. The multitude in the work of Paolo Virno, from this perspective, we argue, should not be considered a strictly political concept, even if it is presented as such within this Italian philosopher's work. It is from out of this excess that is represented by the multitude, anterior to the moment in which politics constitutes itself as subject and object of the foundations of human organisation, that it becomes possible to offer a different orientation with respect to the political sphere. Drawing on ongoing debates which emerged in the context of Latin American Studies in the United States, I will propose to use the name "posthegemony" as the site for such critical reflection on the contemporary conditions of thought and action that does not seek to understand how to reconstitute new forms of political sovereignty but to take a step back from the omnipresence of the political field in contemporary debates, not in order to search for an apolitical or depoliticized register of thought, but precisely in order to repoliticize the political sphere in ways which are non-totalizing.

Thesis One: The world "multitude", as it is found in the work of Paolo Virno specifically, is a way of describing and analyzing our contemporary political moment.

In his work *The Grammar of the Multitude*, Paolo Virno argues for the need to recuperate the concept of the multitude from early modern political theory in order to think about changing social and political conditions associated with transformations in political economy over the last half century. The re-emergence of what he calls the "multitude" is the reappearance of a pre-modern specter which found its most extensive articulation in the work of Thomas Hobbes and Baruch Spinoza (though both of them in very different ways). However, «[in] describing the forms of associative life and of the public spirit of the newly constituted great States», writes

Virno in *The Grammar of the Multitude*, speaking of the rise of political modernity, «one no longer spoke of the multitude, but of people. But we need to ask whether today, at the end of a long cycle, the old dispute has not opened up once again; whether, today, now that the political theory of the modern era is going through a radical crisis, this once defeated notion is not displaying extraordinary vitality, thus taking its dramatic revenge» (2004, p. 21). In what way does the multitude differentiate itself from the people? On a number of occasions, Virno defines the multitude quite simply as the logic of the many, as opposed to the political concept of the "people" which refers to a logic of the "one". He notes that it is the concept of the people and not the multitude that has been given much more extensive analysis and attention throughout the history of political philosophy, and has helped shape and inform the current constitution of the political sphere throughout modernity. In other words, political philosophy has been interested in the logic of the one and not of the many. It is not difficult to detect here a certain critical stance with respect the Western metaphysical tradition and its constitution of politics as a sphere of action in the Heideggerian vein, and inspired by figures such as Jacques Derrida as well as anthropologists such as Pierre Clastres. It is related to what Jacques Rancière has called, in reference to the treatment of politics in Ancient Greek philosophy, the "original scandal of politics": the attempt to find a grounding principle for an originary conflict or *polemos* (Rancière, 1999). By naming politics, political philosophy always seeks to stabilize or contain this conflict, and the scandal of politics is what Rancière identifies as philosophy's own disavowed recognition to be able to do so. Virno is thus concerned with the origins of political theology itself.

For Virno, however, the word "multitude" does not simply name a principle of social agency which resists the tradition of political philosophy to understand politics as a question of the "people" and to reduce the "many" to the "one". The recuperation of the word multitude takes on a very specific function in the work of the Italian philosopher: it is offered primarily as a means for understanding a transformation of the relations of production inherent to the capitalist world-system, and how these transformations simultaneously affect the conditions of political conflict today. It is important to understand that, in distinction to other uses of the term "multitude" in contemporary post-Marxism, the "multitude" does not bear within itself any positive ethical content in Virno's work. «Naturally – writes Virno elsewhere – this metamorphosis has nothing liberatory about it» (1996, p. 202). As a change within the relations of production inherent to the world capitalist system, these transformations must be understood as part of capitalism's ability to reproduce the class system, even if this in turn creates the potential conditions for resistance to capitalist exploitation. The change in these relations of production, alongside the necessary conclusions that Virno draws from them, is not necessarily either positive or negative from Virno's perspective, therefore, though he certainly engages in discussions over certain positive and negative effects. Instead, the "multitude" remains quite simply a means to describe and analyze a contemporary state of affairs under post-Fordist capitalist conditions, where the political logic of the "one" and its containment of political struggle has imploded, and where contemporary political struggle is defined by its multipolarity. The concept of the "multitude", if it is indeed a concept and not actually irreducible to what we commonly understand by conceptuality, plays the function in Virno's work of understanding new conditions of social, political and economic action. This can be explored from a number of different perspectives, but for the sake of economizing on space we will highlight only two here: the transformation of capitalist relations and the subsequent collapse of the grand narratives of modernity.

The recuperation of the word "multitude" is taken up in Virno's work in order to understand, primarily, a transformation of the relations of production inherent to the capitalist world-system. One of the important changes in this respect is with regards to the spheres of social action. Virno draws from linguistic theory in order to propose that changes in the conditions of production under the post-Fordist industrial model has resulted in the general substitution of what he calls "special places" for "common places". Whereas under the Fordist model of production, different spheres of action were clearly contained within specific domains (politics was the domain of the party, education was the domain of the school and the university, work was the domain of the factory, etc.), in the post-Fordist model it is the fact of linguistic understanding itself which becomes the domain of and the raw material for all of these once separate spheres of action, now much more difficult to distinguish or contain. The real subsumption of labour to capital as it is given in the new models of bio-technology and the extension of labour to all spheres of human life has produced the generalisation and totalisation of labour as an abstraction of human action and productivity. A generalisation and totalisation of labour, however, is at the same time a generalisation and totalisation of politics (nowhere is this clearer, perhaps, than in the configuration of contemporary liberal parliamentary democracies, where politicians increasingly operate as technocrats whose "job" it is to maintain international consensus and economic stability). This phenomenon which sees the general extension of capitalist relations of production across all domains of human life being captured by technologies of communication is what Antonio Negri has identified with the name of the General Social Intellect. This General Intellect is the place which gives the "multitude" its unity, according to Virno, unlike the case of the "people" whose unity was found in the state. However, Virno arguably goes a step further than Negri in his analysis of this General Intellect insofar as he demonstrates how this transformation turns the intellect itself from the most private activity, as it was in Hannah Arendt's *The Human Condition*, to the most public of activities, making indistinguishable those three separate spheres of action that for Hannah Arendt defined human action: labour, action and thought (i.e. intellect). What Hannah Arendt had identified as "necessarily" the most private of human activities – thought or the activity of the intellect – becomes the most public kind of activity in the age of the multitude. The distinction between work and action becomes redundant; political action is already a question of productivity and productivity is already a question of political action (challenging the Aristotelian distinctions between *poeisis* and *praxis* which were still self-evident for Arendt).

This transformation in the conditions of capitalist production is therefore more than a question of labour; it is a transformation in the contemporary forms of social action and their possibilities, changes, indeed, to the forms of life itself (giving thus Virno the subtitle to his book on the grammar of the multitude). Indeed, one of the most salient features that Virno has commented upon regarding his theory for a grammar of the multitude is the notion that this change in the type of production has led to a collapse of a series of narratives which had appeared to be perfectly sustainable and self-evident under political modernity. One of these narratives which collapses in the age of the multitude and the General Social Intellect is the distinction between the private and the public spheres, given that it is the ability of linguistic communication itself and the (once private) intellect that becomes the source of both (once private) productivity and (once public) action. The distinction in Marx, which was always possible in principle, between real labour and abstract labour becomes an impossible fantasy in the age of the multitude. As has been commented by other philosophers, this collapse in the distinction between the private and public sphere is intimately connected to the problematic of biopolitics today, and is self-evident in our multiple engagements with "social media" networks in which the abstraction of the human self as the labour of mediated technologies and of the intellect is clearly demonstrated.

If we are to accept Virno's diagnosis of the current conditions of capitalist production in the post-Fordist model, I believe that it has a number of important consequences which have still to be properly explored, and which I will not have the time to discuss in any detail here. The first of these that I shall only mention in passing is that Virno's model can offer potential ways of understanding the centre of class conflict today, even if Virno himself rarely speaks in such terms. By focusing on contemporary production as "virtuosic" and bringing in the metaphor of musical performance as «the production of communication by means of communication» (2004, p. 56), Virno necessarily introduces an important distinction that is very clear in the case of musical performance between the writing of the score and its performance. As in multimodal semiotics, where Gunther Kress and Theo Van Leeuwan (2016) have made an important distinction between design on the one hand and production or delivery on the other, one might be tempted to put forward that the new proletariat today continues to be those who only own their own capacity for labour value; however, in the post-Fordist model, this is now expressed as a difference between those who have the power to influence the forms that the General Intellect can take ("design") versus those who only have the power to implement those forms or follow those models ("production") which are set and institutionalised by others. Increasingly, today, this distinction depends on the capacity to have access to and manipulate those technological and communicative platforms which determine our interaction with one another.

Another important consequence of Virno's analysis is that the General Intellect itself becomes the unifying force of the "many" that the multitude represents. But what is important about this is that this "many" nevertheless never ceases to be "many". In other words, the multitude for Virno is not a narrative which articulates the many *as* the one, but rather simply a means to assess the structure of a new human condition, or, perhaps, the undoing of a previously self-evident basis for understanding humanity which has not been replaced by any single master narrative. He describes the General Intellect in this sense as a «non-public public sphere, a *non-governmental* public sphere, far from the myths and rituals of sovereignty» (2004, p. 40, Virno's emphasis). The unity of the multitude is no longer the state, he writes, as it was in the case of the people; «rather, it is language, intellect, the communal faculties of the human race» (p. 25). But is this kind of unity offered by the multitude and the General Intellect really the same kind of unity that was offered in political modernity by the state? According to Virno himself, the difference lies in the fact that this unity is not something towards which things converge, not a centre of gravity that draws heterogenous elements into a general principle, but a kind of precondition, an individualisation of the universal experience. The multitude thus comes prior to the possibility of political articulation, of the attempt to suture this heterogenous realm which is never totalizable insofar as it is defined by multipolarity. Curiously, in precisely the moment in which Virno offers the multitude as a form for explaining the totalisation of the political sphere, which now interpenetrates all realms of human life, indeed, takes human life ("the communal faculties of the human race") as its source of production, he simultaneously offers the concept of the multitude as a sphere of heterogeneity and irreducibility which is a precondition to political action, and therefore anterior to politics itself as the totalization of the social field.

Thesis Two: The multitude is not a political concept

Strictly speaking, therefore, we suggest that the multitude cannot be considered to refer to something "political", even if it has been used that way in some contemporary political theory. What the term seeks to describe should be considered un-political, or perhaps "infra-political", in nature. This is not to say that the multitude is a passive, non-actor, but it refers to a heterogeneity, to a possibility of action which will always resist hegemonic and political articulation, and cannot itself be given a form of re-presentation because it defies by its very nature the logic of presence. Such a thesis may seem at first sight surprising, given that the most common formulation of the multitude in Antonio Negri and Michael Hardt's work consistently sees the multitude as the locus of new political action. But the conversion of the multitude from a disperse set of claims to a united political group remains speculative in Hardt and Negri's work and there seems to be no obvious solution to this problem. Although Jon Beasley-Murray's well-known use of the language of the multitude to explain the term "posthegemony" draws from Hardt and Negri, he is overtly critical of the move by which, in his words, «[with] the declaration that communism is immanent, analysis shades into project» (2010, p. 281). The multitude as a political "project", therefore, leads us nowhere except to the old philosophical fantasy of the end of politics, traceable throughout political philosophy from Plato through to Marx. Yet, as Sylvère Lontringer notes in her introduction to the *Grammar of the Multitude*, Virno's notion takes on no such normative dimension: «Unlike Hardt and Negri, Virno refrains from turning exile, or the multitude for that matter, let alone communism, into another splendid myth» (2004, p. 9). Virno describes the logic of the many as one that, precisely because it remains many and is never reducible to the one, is "un-representable". The multitude escapes any logic of re-presentation, and therefore must necessarily, I suggest, be understood as escaping any metaphysics of presence whatsoever. It is what takes place "in spite of" political articulation. Something else is going on, then, or is at stake, in the multitude. It is impossible to make a hegemonic principle out of the multitude without whatever we refer to with this word dissolving itself in the same instance.

I am drawing in part here from observations made by Giorgio Agamben on the notions of the "people" and the "multitude" in Thomas Hobbes's *Leviathan*. Analysing the emblematic frontispiece of the work, where the mythical creature of the Leviathan is presented as a body composed of bodies, Agamben discusses the problem of the multitude in Hobbes as an ocular question and as a figure of the imagination. Agamben reminds us in his analysis of the frontispiece in his essay *Stasis* of Hobbes's own interest in the advancement in the science of optics at the time. He shows Hobbes to draw from these lessons from optics in his thinking about how the state comes into being as a kind of optical illusion. It is from this interpretation of Hobbes's frontispiece as an optical play that Agamben is able to conclude that the multitude in Hobbes «has no political significance» (2015, p. 37), but is actually part of an optical illusion in which the multitude must disappear to the eye in order for the state to come into being; that is, to become visible or imaginable. The multitude is, from this perspective, «the unpolitical element upon whose exclusion the city is founded» (*ibid.*). We should not forget that it is precisely this unpolitical element which Agamben identifies with the subject of civil war. The multitude therefore forms part of an ocular politics which must be policed and cared for in order for the image, fantasy or appearance of the state to be maintained, and it is this caring and policing which forms part of the foundations of a biopolitical regime. «While perfectly illustrating the paradoxical status of the Hobbesian multitude," writes Agamben, "the emblem of the frontispiece is also a courier that announces the biopolitical turn that sovereign power was preparing to make» (p. 38). This policing is not only a policing of the political body (and of those bodies who occupy the political space), but of the sensory apparatus itself, by means of which, like a magical illusion, the unpolitical multitude could become and maintain itself as the political people without this ever guaranteeing the political stability of the city, and therefore constantly threatening to overflow it in the form of civil war. Agamben further notes that in today's world where the political space has become the space of economic management and policing, the form that civil war takes is terrorism. Agamben's reflections here coincide with the post-Schmittian reflections of other philosophers such as Carlo Galli, who draws on the figure of the terrorist in the post-9/11 world to discuss the reconfiguration of contemporary political conflict, which is no longer contained to the friend-enemy dichotomy contained by the nation-state (Galli, 2010).

Thesis Three: A return to the 'People' is neither possible nor desirable.

The urgent question for us today in light of the previous observations is therefore the following: how are we to respond today to the "return of the multitude" on the contemporary political scene? We should be reminded in this sense that unlike in the work of Hardt and Negri where the multitude is championed as the possibility for new revolutionary action and a new form of communism, through Virno's work we prefer to understand the multitude as the reconfiguration of capitalist relations which has resulted in a number of serious crises which have both conceptual and political dimensions. In the political domain, the most serious symptom of this general crisis is the collapse of a political model which emerged through struggle throughout the seventeenth and eighteenth centuries in particular and throughout the nineteenth century became hegemonic: the rise of the nation-state and its embodiment in the "People" (with a capital "P" to emphasize the indivisibility of political sovereignty that this notion presupposes). Against the current talk of crisis of the nation-state and apocalyptic visions that fill our current cultural narratives, however, we wish to suggest that a return to the "People" (with a capital "P") is neither possible nor desirable. The exclusionary nature of the nation-state apparatus, what it presupposed for categories of race, normality, criminality, delinquency, and its instrumental means of maintaining class relations, has been commented upon at great length in the work of many scholars from across numerous disciplines over the previous half century. Without celebrating the end of the great era of the nation-state as the opening onto some kind of anarchic paradise (we must recognize the new threats that emerge in the form of international policing and the proliferation of spaces that Giorgio Agamben has identified with the name of the "camp" or zones of exception to the law), we must not give into the temptation of harking back to an imagined time of peace, stability or consensus which was based on a phantasmatic notion of national homogeneity. There is no revival of the Leviathan at least while we are still living in its shadow. The impossibility of making a hegemonic principle out of the multitude without the multitude dissolving in the same instance does not mean that the solution is a return to the fantasy of the political community of the *arche*. The "return of the multitude" must therefore have some significance other than telling us about the impending catastrophe of a world conflict without *katechon*. How can the "unpolitical" multitude become today the object of political reflection, and what would this mean for the way in which we think about politics?

Thesis Four: The "politics of the multitude" is the name I propose to give to the current responses that we see today to this political crisis.

The "politics of the multitude" is the name I propose to give to the current political responses that we see today to our political crisis, which is a crisis of the Leviathan model, that is to say of the liberal state. This "response" developed out of the global communication technologies associated with the General Intellect and can perhaps be understood as taking place in two phases: the first as new social movements which came together under various names, often invoking an ambiguous notion of the commons (the Occupy movement in the United States and the 15-M in Spain being two emblematic examples), and a second by anti-establishment political movements that have sought to channel this generalised discontent being expressed through new media channels, often going under the name of "populism". From this perspective, and as I have argued in more detail elsewhere (Baker, 2017), it is possible to argue that the Laclauian version of hegemony is a modality of political action adapted to the question of how one carries out political action today. This would not be the creation of the "People" (with a capital "P", presupposing the indivisibility of sovereignty), not the restoration of the Leviathan model in other words, but the creation of a multiplicity of "peoples" (with small "p") from out of the new conditions of action described by the use of the word "multitude" (which also means, I would insist, the derivation of something political out of something else which itself is not strictly speaking political). In his work, particularly for example in his *On Populist Reason* (2005), Laclau explicitly expresses his notion of hegemony as the making of a narrative from out of the collapse of grand narratives; as the actualization of possibilities latent within the social seen as a motley assortment of elements, the ruins of a former coherent narrative of modernity. He emphasizes time and again that there is no full suturing of the social space, and that the hegemonic game is formed of democratic and popular forms. Political identities in Laclau's work are always multiple and multipolar; hegemony is not hegemony of the "state" in Laclau, as it is in Gramsci, even if this means that Laclau is sometimes blind to larger questions of political economy which take a much more prominent work in the writings of the Italian philosopher. Contemporary populisms, even when they speak in nationalist terms, cannot be immediately understood as the restoration of a hegemonic model of the nation-state of nineteenth century bourgeois liberalism.

Thesis Five: Populism is therefore not only a way of constructing the people; it also describes a mode of action appropriate to the postmodern and post-Fordist conditions that the idea of "multitude" attempts to express.

I believe that this thesis is already self-evident in Laclau's own elaboration of hegemony theory as an all-encompassing theory of the social. In his own words, Laclau is not a political scientist but a political ontologist: he analyzes the very emergence of political forms as such. We accept of course all of the criticisms that have been laid against Laclau in terms of the limitations of hegemony theory. I suggest that the innovation of my thesis on Laclau's populism (and all practices that can be derived from it) is not that Laclau claims to give us a comprehensive theory of the social and the political, but rather that, in understanding hegemony as a practice of articulations, he brings hegemony theory up-to-date to fit a specific kind of praxis compatible with a world in which the fact of communication itself has become the raw material of capitalist accumulation: that is, a world where the General Intellect takes centre stage. Laclau's theory of hegemony "as" populism is therefore a "politics of the multitude": a way of engaging in political action in an age defined by the characteristics we listed above (there are no doubt other types of this practice that we could identify today, but for a lack of space we will concentrate only on the theory of populism in Ernesto Laclau). This technique and praxis is redefining the game of politics, as evidenced by the numerous populist practices on the left that draw on theories of hegemony in order to theorise and justify their own practices. More than acceding to the inevitability of new populisms today, however, what this tells us about is a new kind of action and organisation which can no longer be contained by the liberal state and thus is in urgent need of analysis.

The question that we are forced to raise is thus: does populism as a "politics of the multitude" provide the appropriate horizon for all future political thought and action in today's current configuration of social relations and power? Although it seems to me that an engagement with contemporary populism and its significance is inevitable, at the same time I believe that this is on its own insufficient for analysing and thinking through contemporary conditions of social action. The complexity of the issue that Paolo Virno has attempted to outline in his work runs deeper than this. If the "return of the multitude" is also the emergence of a world where conflict is multi-polar, if there is no single narrative or geometry from which to rebuilt a principle of our belonging-together, then how are we to rethink categories of thought and action which do not seek to simply restore the security and comfortability of a *mythos*-turned-truth (with the inevitable violence that this "white mythology" would entail?). What are contemporary struggles a struggle over, if not hegemony, remembering always that hegemony is the imposition of one person's convenient world vision over everyone else's?

Thesis Six: The struggle today is not over hegemony, but also over the possibility of what it means to act and to think, beyond any single political narrative.

My essential argument is the following: the current forms of the "politics of the multitude" miss the point that the struggle today is not "only" over hegemony, but also over the very possibility of what it means to act, to engage with one another, about habits and about interactions which exceed any single, political narrative. Indeed, "missing the point" may be in fact too limited an expression, when in fact the current "politics of the multitude", insofar as they can be understood as techniques through which to cultivate and harness the current conditions of political action, are oftentimes ideological cover-ups for a continued alliance with capitalist forms and of the maintenance of power-relations, as contemporary populisms in Spain, Latin America and elsewhere have shown in recent years (which is not to say that those forms of capitalism or power relations are not preferable to the neoliberal types which preceded them; the point is, however, that they do not offer any real threat to the capitalist accumulation of which they rhetorically present themselves as enemies). This question over what it means to act is perhaps most apparent today in the crisis of political forms in formerly colonized nations. In Bolivia and Ecuador, perhaps two of the most radical constitutional experiments in recent Latin American history, it is clear that the idea of a Plurinational State which is able to be a home to both modern and indigenous forms of political, social and economic organization, it is not any single narrative that will make this possible, but an entirely different way of thinking about what it means to distribute sovereignty, to organize, in other words, the interactions between different layers of society, each with entirely different and even opposing ways of thinking about relationships to the land and sovereignty. Perhaps the very possibility of bringing to an end the legacy of European colonialisms in "post-colonial" nations, of how to bring an end to imperial and capitalist domination of what still remains the legacy of the expansion of Western forms of power across the world (bourgeois liberal capitalism), lies in this question about how to think about the significance of the "politics of the multitude" today.

Thesis Seven: "Posthegemony" is the term which thematizes this issue.

I suggest the reservation of the term "posthegemony" as quite simply the thematisation of this issue. It is therefore any practice of the "politics of the multitude" that seeks not to construct a principle of hegemony, but instead to rethink and reorganise the very principles of political action upon which the modern tradition is based, in order to think beyond the restitution of hegemony. This definition does not need to be prescriptive, and I would like to separate this statement from anything might be said more specifically under the name of posthegemony elsewhere. In other words, I would not like to keep the name posthegemony for a specific way of thematising this issue or acting, which would instead be theories or practices placed in a posthegemonic mode. This way, the word "posthegemony" can delimit a critical perspective on the present which can be used without necessarily agreeing with the specifics of what has been said under its name, for example by Jon Beasley-Murray, Gareth Williams or Alberto Moreiras who have probably given it its most explicit thematisation, although each in very different ways. Instead, it can become a problematic and a space of common dialogue that attempts to move beyond the common sense notions of politics which continue to blind us to the complexity of the challenges we face today, in the shadow of the Leviathan.

References

Agamben G. (2015). *Stasis: Civil War as a Political Paradigm.* Stanford: Stanford University Press.
Baker P. (2017). (Post)Hegemony and the Promise of Populism: Reflections on the Politics of Our Times. *Política Común.* 10. Online: <https://quod.lib.umich.edu/p/pc/12322227.0010.002/-post-hegemony-and-the-promise-of-populism-reflections?keywords=...;rgn=main;view=fulltext> (Accessed 4 June 2018).
Beasley-Murray J. (2010). *Posthegemony: Political Theory and Latin America.* Minneapolis: Minnesota University Press.
Errejón Í. (2017). Occidente en su momento populista. *Revista Contexto.* 22 April. Online: <http://ctxt.es/es/20170419/Firmas/12306/populismo-izquierda-errejon-le-pen-trump.htm.> (Accessed: 4 June 2018)
Galli C. (2010). *Political Spaces and Global War.* Minneapolis: University of Minnesota Press.
Kress G. and Van Leeuwan T. (2016). *Multimodal Discourse: The Modes and Media of Contemporary Communication.* London: Hodder Education.
Laclau E. (2005). *On Populist Reason.* New York: Verso.
Lotringer S. (2004). Foreword: We, the Multitude. In: *A Grammar of the Multitude: For an Analysis of Contemporary Forms of Life.* New York: Semiotext(e): 7-19.
Rancière J. (1999). *Disagreement: Politics and Philosophy.* Minneapolis: University of Minnesota Press.
Virno P. (2004). *A Grammar of the Multitude: For an Analysis of Contemporary Forms of Life.* New York: Semiotext(e).
Virno P. (1996). Virtuosity and Revolution: The Political Theory of Exodus. In: Paolo V. and Michael Hardt M., eds. *Radical Thought in Italy: A Potential Politics.* Minneapolis: University of Minnesota Press: 13-37.

MIMESIS GROUP
www.mimesis-group.com

MIMESIS INTERNATIONAL
www.mimesisinternational.com
info@mimesisinternational.com

MIMESIS EDIZIONI
www.mimesisedizioni.it
mimesis@mimesisedizioni.it

ÉDITIONS MIMÉSIS
www.editionsmimesis.fr
info@editionsmimesis.fr

MIMESIS COMMUNICATION
www.mim-c.net

MIMESIS EU
www.mim-eu.com

Printed by
Geca Industrie Grafiche – San Giuliano Milanese (MI)
September 2020